CuR
510
EM/6
2004

P9-ARQ-929

Sixth Grade

Everyday Mathematics®

Assessment Handbook

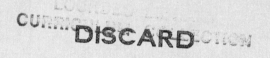

Gwynedd-Mercy College
P.O. Box 901
Gwynedd Valley, PA 19437-0901

DISCARD

CURRICULUM COLLECTION

DISCARD

cuR
510
Em/6
2004

Sixth Grade

Everyday Mathematics®

Assessment Handbook

Lourdes Library
Gwynedd-Mercy College
P. O. Box 901
Gwynedd Valley, PA 19437-0901

The University of Chicago School Mathematics Project

LOURDES LIBRARY
CURRICULUM COLLECTION

The McGraw-Hill Companies

UCSMP Elementary Materials Component

Max Bell, Director

Authors
Jean Bell
William M. Carroll

Photo Credits
Cover: Bill Burlingham/Photography
Photo Collage: Herman Adler Design

Contributers
Ellen Dairyko, Amy Dillard, Sharon Draznin,
Nancy Hanvey, Laurie Leff, Denise Porter,
Herb Price, Joyce Timmons, Lisa Winters

 **Wright Group**

Copyright © 2004 by Wright Group/McGraw-Hill.

All rights reserved. Except as permitted under the United States
Copyright Act, no part of this publication may be reproduced or
distributed in any form or by any means, or stored in a database
or retrieval system, without the prior written permission from the
publisher, unless otherwise indicated.

Printed in the United States of America.

Send all inquiries to:
Wright Group/McGraw-Hill
P.O. Box 812960
Chicago, IL 60681

ISBN 0-07-600066-4

5 6 7 8 9 10 11 POH 09 08 07 06 05

The *McGraw-Hill* Companies

Contents

Introduction

Too often, school assessment is equated with testing and grading. While some formal assessment is necessary, it tends to provide only scattered snapshots of students' performance rather than records of their growth and progress. The philosophy of *Everyday Mathematics®* is that real assessment should be more like a motion picture, revealing the development of the student's mathematical understanding while giving the teacher useful feedback about instructional needs. Rather than simply providing tests on isolated skills, *Everyday Mathematics* offers a variety of useful techniques and opportunities to assess students' progress on skills, concepts, and thinking processes.

Several assessment tools are built into the *Everyday Mathematics* program. Slate assessments and end-of-unit written assessments are useful in showing how well students are learning the concepts and skills covered in a unit. But these tools by themselves do not provide a balance, highlight progress, or show students' work on larger problems. The purpose of this handbook is to broaden your assessment techniques. Rather than using all of the techniques suggested here, choose a few that balance written work with observation, individual work with group work, and short answers with longer explanations.

For assessment to be valid and useful to both teachers and students, the authors believe that

- teachers need to have a variety of assessment tools and techniques from which to choose.
- students should be included in the assessment process through interviews, written work, and conferences that provide appropriate feedback. Self-assessment and reflection are skills that will develop over time if encouraged.
- assessment and instruction should be closely linked. Assessment should assist teachers in making instructional decisions concerning both individual students and the whole class.
- a good assessment plan makes instruction easier.
- the best assessment plans are those developed by teachers working collaboratively within their schools.

♦ Math Masters, p. 476

This handbook compiles classroom-tested techniques used by experienced *Everyday Mathematics* teachers. It includes suggestions for observing students, keeping anecdotal records, following student progress, and encouraging students to reflect on and communicate both what they have learned and how they feel about mathematics. Many of the assessment suggestions are aimed specifically at *Everyday Mathematics* activities, such as using partner activities and games to observe students and using Math Boxes to focus on a particular concept or skill.

As you read through this handbook, you may want to start with one or two activities that fit your needs and assist you in building a balanced approach to assessment. Feel free to adapt the materials to your own needs. While some teachers find math logs useful, others find observations and short, informal interviews more helpful.

The *Everyday Mathematics* goal is to furnish you with some ideas to make assessment and instruction more manageable, productive, and exciting; as well as offer you a more complete picture of each student's progress and instructional needs.

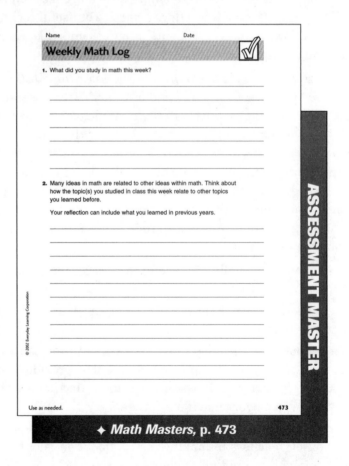

✦ *Math Masters, p. 473*

A Balance of Assessments

Ongoing, Product, and Periodic Assessments, and Outside Tests

Although there is no one "right" assessment plan for all classrooms, all assessment plans should use a variety of techniques. To develop your own plan, consider four different assessment sources within the Quad shown in the figure below.

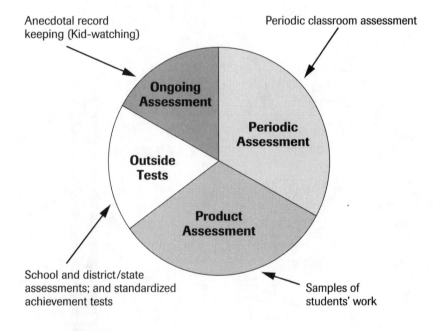

Anecdotal record keeping (Kid-watching)

Periodic classroom assessment

Ongoing Assessment

Periodic Assessment

Outside Tests

Product Assessment

School and district/state assessments; and standardized achievement tests

Samples of students' work

The content of this handbook provides further details about the assessment sources shown in the circle graph. Your own assessment plan should answer these questions:

- *How is the class doing as a whole?*
- *How are individual students doing?*
- *How do I need to adjust instructions to meet students' needs?*
- *How can I communicate to students, parents, and others about the progress being made?*

The proportions of assessment sources shown in the circle graph are quite flexible and depend on a number of factors, such as experience of the students and time of year. At the beginning of the year, teachers might use a higher proportion of Ongoing and Product Assessment sources with smaller proportions of Periodic and Outside Test sources.

The section beginning on page 37 provides for each unit examples of how to use different types of assessments in specific lessons.

Ongoing Assessment includes observations of student involvement in regular classroom activities, such as working with partners or small groups during games and working individually on Math Boxes. It may also include observations of students' thinking and shared strategies and information you gather from classroom interactions or from informal individual interviews. Records of these ongoing assessments may take the form of short, written notes; more elaborate record pages; or brief mental notes to yourself. See Ongoing Assessment, pages 15 and 16, for details.

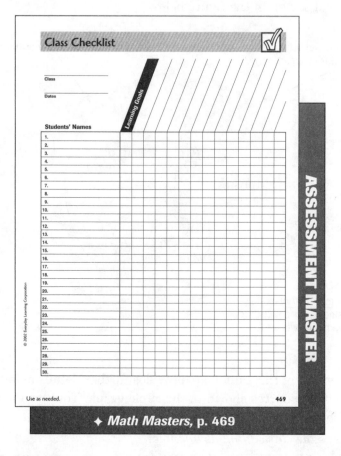

♦ *Math Masters*, p. 469

Product Assessment may include samples of Math Boxes, journal pages, Study Links, solutions to open-ended problems, group project reports, mathematical writing, drawings, sketches, diagrams, and anything else you feel has value and reflects what you want learners to do. If you are keeping portfolios, students should help select which products to include. See Portfolios, pages 7–11, and Product Assessment, pages 17–22.

Periodic Assessment includes more formal assessments, such as end-of-unit assessments, cumulative reviews, quizzes, Class Progress Indicators, and math interest inventories. Pages 23–29 offer suggestions and extensions intended to help you measure both individual and class progress using these types of assessment.

Outside Tests provide information from school, district, state, and standardized tests that might be used to evaluate the progress of a student, class, or school. See page 33 for more information.

A List of Assessment Sources attached to students' folders or portfolios or kept in your record book may help you see whether you have included information from the first three sources of the Quad as well as from other sources. Notice that the completed sample shown below includes only a few of the assessment suggestions from each source. Another teacher might choose other entries. Using multiple techniques will give you a clear picture of each student's progress and instructional needs.

Use this List of Assessment Sources master to keep track of the assessment sources that you are currently using. A blank sample is provided as *Math Masters,* page 467, and is shown in reduced form on page 113 of this book.

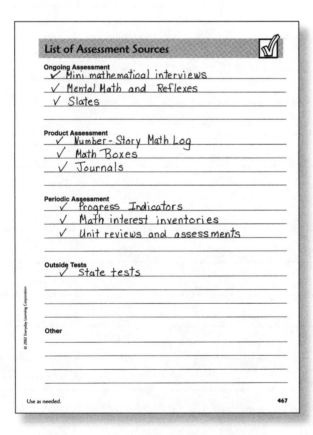

List of Assessment Sources

Ongoing Assessment
✓ Mini mathematical interviews
✓ Mental Math and Reflexes
✓ Slates

Product Assessment
✓ Number-Story Math Log
✓ Math Boxes
✓ Journals

Periodic Assessment
✓ Progress Indicators
✓ Math interest inventories
✓ Unit reviews and assessments

Outside Tests
✓ State tests

Other

Use as needed.   467

© 2002 Everyday Learning Corporation

NOTE: Do not try to use all assessment sources at once. Instead, devise a manageable, balanced plan.

Your assessment plan should answer these questions:
- *How is the class performing as a whole?*
- *How are individual students performing?*
- *How can I adjust instruction to meet students' needs?*
- *How can I communicate to students, parents, and others about the progress being made?*

Your Assessment Ideas

_____

_____

_____

_____

_____

_____

_____

_____

_____

_____

_____

_____

_____

_____

_____

_____

_____

_____

_____

_____

_____

_____

_____

_____

_____

_____

_____

Your Assessment Ideas

Portfolios

Using Portfolios

Portfolios are used for a number of different purposes, from keeping track of progress to helping students become more reflective about their mathematical growth. The practice of keeping portfolios is a positive assessment technique and is consistent with the philosophy of *Everyday Mathematics* for the following reasons:

- Portfolios emphasize progress over time, rather than results at a given moment. At any time, a student may have Beginning, Developing, or Secure understandings of various mathematical concepts. This progress can best be exhibited by a collection of products organized into portfolios or folders that contain work from different contexts and from different times in the year.

- Portfolios can involve students more directly in the assessment process. Students may write introductions and help select portfolio entries. They can select work they are especially proud of and tag each piece with an explanation of why it was chosen. Developing realistic self-assessment is a valuable skill that takes time to acquire.

- Portfolios can be used as evidence of progress for students, their families, and their teachers for next year. You may want to establish a "Portfolio Night" for students and their parents to attend in order to allow them time to discuss and review portfolio contents. It is very important that parents understand the goals of the various projects and assignments.

- Portfolios can illustrate students' strengths and weaknesses in particular areas of mathematics. Since a rich body of work can be contained in a portfolio, it is a good vehicle for exhibiting each student's progress. Portfolios also can be used to assess students' abilities to see connections within mathematics and to apply mathematical ideas to real-world situations.

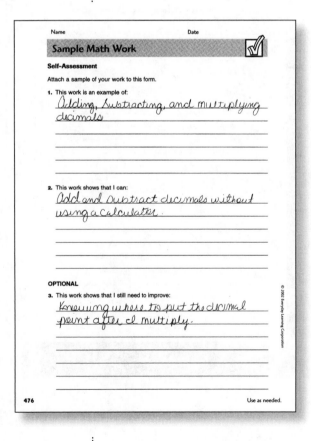

Some teachers keep two types of portfolios: a working portfolio in which students store their recent work and an assessment portfolio. Occasionally, a selection of work is transferred from the working portfolio to the assessment portfolio. Usually, the teacher provides some guidelines for what should be selected, allowing learners to choose within these guidelines.

Many teachers recommend that the number of entries in an assessment portfolio be limited. These entries provide a manageable but representative sample of work. New work can replace old, but some samples from throughout the year should remain.

Listed below are some ideas of representative work that might be included in such a portfolio:

- End-of-unit assessments
- Key assignments
- Student's solutions to challenging problems
- Written accounts of student's feelings about mathematics
- Drawings, sketches, and representations of mathematical ideas and situations
- Photographs of students engaging in mathematics
- Videotapes of students communicating mathematically

For more guidance on developing portfolio assessment, you may wish to consult one of several excellent sources listed on page 35. We especially recommend *Mathematics Assessment: Myths, Models, Good Questions, and Practical Suggestions,* edited by Jean Kerr Stenmark, available through the National Council of Teachers of Mathematics (NCTM). Portfolios, as well as other assessment issues, are also frequently addressed in the NCTM journal *Teaching Children Mathematics.* A video available from NCTM, *Mathematics Assessment: Alternative Approaches,* also discusses portfolios and may be helpful for teachers who are working together to develop a school-wide assessment policy.

Name _____ Date _____

Discussion of My Math Work

Self-Assessment

Attach a sample of your work to this page. Tell what you think is important about your sample.

Use as needed. 477

ASSESSMENT MASTER

© 2002 Everyday Learning Corporation

✦ *Math Masters, p. 477*

Ideas in the *Teacher's Lesson Guide*

Portfolio Ideas Samples of students' work may be obtained from the following assignments:

Unit 1

- Creating and Analyzing a Mystery Line Plot **(Lesson 1.2)**
- Completing Name-Collection Boxes **(Lesson 1.3)**
- Making Bar Graphs **(Lesson 1.6)**
- Reading Circle Graphs **(Lesson 1.8)**
- Solving a Paint Problem **(Lesson 1.9)**
- Creating Persuasive Graphs **(Lesson 1.10)**
- Correcting a Misleading Pictograph **(Lesson 1.10)**
- Collecting and Analyzing Data **(Lesson 1.11)**
- Report on Collected Graphs **(Lesson 1.12)**

Unit 2

- Writing Decimal Number Stories **(Lesson 2.1)**
- Finding Exponential Notation in Data **(Lesson 2.7)**
- Comparing Ground Areas of Famous Buildings **(Lesson 2.8)**
- Describe a Decimal Computation Strategy **(Lesson 2.12)**

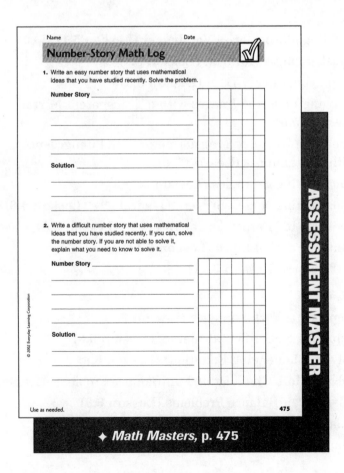

◆ *Math Masters*, p. 475

Unit 3

- Finding True and Not True Special Cases (**Lesson 3.2**)
- Deriving a Brick-Wall Formula (**Lesson 3.4**)
- Writing Number Stories Involving Rates (**Lesson 3.5**)
- Conducting a Ball-Throwing Experiment (**Lesson 3.6**)
- Constructing Mystery Graphs (**Lesson 3.9**)
- Evaluate Formulas (**Lesson 3.11**)
- Interpret Mystery Graphs (**Lesson 3.11**)

Unit 4

- Exploring the Egyptian Method of Writing Fractions (**Lesson 4.3**)
- Exploring Zeno's Paradox (**Lesson 4.3**)
- Practicing Mixed-Number Multiplication (**Lesson 4.7**)
- Collecting Survey Data and Displaying Them in a Circle Graph (**Lesson 4.10**)
- Taking and Interpreting a Survey (**Lesson 4.11**)
- Write and Solve Fraction Number Stories (**Lesson 4.12**)
- Describe a Fraction or Mixed-Number Computation Strategy (**Lesson 4.12**)

Unit 5

- Building Mathematics Vocabulary (**Lesson 5.1**)
- Constructing a Hexagon (**Lesson 5.1**)
- Displaying Survey Data (**Lesson 5.3**)
- Drawing Reflected Images with a Transparent Mirror (**Lesson 5.5**)
- Exploring Isometry Transformations and Congruence with Pentaminoes (**Lesson 5.6**)
- Constructing Triangles (**Lesson 5.7**)
- Constructing Non-Congruent Quadrangles (**Lesson 5.8**)
- Constructing Perpendicular Bisectors (**Lesson 5.8**)
- Identify Parallel Lines (**Lesson 5.11**)
- Sort Shapes (**Lesson 5.11**)

Unit 6

- Completing Fact Triangles (**Lesson 6.4**)
- Exploring Scientific Calculators (**Lesson 6.6**)
- Solving Challenging Equations (**Lesson 6.8**)
- Solving More Challenging Pan-Balance Problems (**Lesson 6.9**)
- Solving Pan-Balance Problems (**Lesson 6.9**)
- Balancing Pans (**Lesson 6.10**)
- Graphing Inequalities (**Lesson 6.12**)

Unit 7

- Playing Carnival Games **(Lesson 7.1)**
- Running an Amazing Contest **(Lesson 7.4)**
- Improving Scores on Multiple Choice Tests **(Lesson 7.8)**
- Make a Fair Game **(Lesson 7.9)**
- Make Venn Diagrams from Internet Searches **(Lesson 7.9)**

Unit 8

- Calculating Amounts of Ingredients for Making Peanut Butter Fudge **(Lesson 8.3)**
- Making a Circle Graph to Represent a Meal **(Lesson 8.5)**
- Using a Grid to Draw an Enlargement of a Picture **(Lesson 8.10)**
- Reducing Designs **(Lesson 8.10)**
- Reading Ratios **(Lesson 8.11)**
- Calculate Amounts of Ingredients **(Lesson 8.13)**
- Write Ratio Number Stories **(Lesson 8.13)**
- Enlarge a Picture **(Lesson 8.13)**

Unit 9

- Finding the Area of Rectangles **(Lesson 9.1)**
- Interpreting an Algebra Cartoon **(Lesson 9.3)**
- Using Formulas to Complete a Spreadsheet **(Lesson 9.7)**
- Calculating Floor Space **(Lesson 9.8)**
- Writing Volume and Area Number Stories **(Lesson 9.11)**
- Investigating the Pythagorean Theorem **(Lesson 9.12)**
- Write Number Stories Involving the Distributive Property **(Lesson 9.14)**
- Interpret an Algebra Cartoon **(Lesson 9.14)**
- Explore the Area of Parallelograms and Triangles **(Lesson 9.14)**

Unit 10

- Exploring Regular Tessellations **(Lesson 10.1)**
- Drawing Shapes with Rotation Symmetry of a Given Order **(Lesson 10.3)**

◆ *Math Masters*, p. 148

Your Assessment Ideas

_____

_____

_____

_____

_____

_____

_____

_____

_____

_____

_____

_____

_____

_____

_____

_____

_____

_____

_____

_____

_____

_____

_____

_____

_____

_____

Your Assessment Ideas

Rubrics

As most teachers know, learning and understanding are ongoing processes. One good way to keep track of each student's progress is to use a rubric. A rubric is a framework that helps you categorize progress on various aspects of a student's learning. A simple but effective rubric that many teachers use is the classification of students as Beginning, Developing, or Secure with respect to a particular skill or concept. The following rubrics are provided as an introduction to this topic. The most effective rubrics will be those that you and your fellow grade-level teachers tailor to the needs of your students and to the content you are covering.

Sample Rubric
Beginning (B) Students' responses have fragments of appropriate material and show effort to accomplish the task. Students do not explain either the concepts or procedures involved.
Developing (D) Students accomplish part of the task independently. Students can partially explain the process but may need prompting to complete it.
Secure (S) Students' strategies and executions meet the demands of the task and demonstrate a firm grasp of the concepts and procedures involved. Their responses also demonstrate a broad range of understanding, and students apply their understanding in different contexts.

Your own rubric can be modeled after the sample but tailored to meet individual tasks. The sample rubric above can be easily used with any of the sample assessment tools to keep track of the progress of individual students as well as the whole class. You may wish to use the symbols B, D, and S or another set of symbols, such as −, ✓, and +, to chart progress. One teacher suggests using red, yellow, and green color symbols. No matter which rubric symbols you use, a quick look at a completed Class Checklist or a Class Progress Indicator can tell you which areas need further review or which students will benefit from additional help or challenges.

Because some students fall between Developing and Secure or may show exemplary understanding, a 3-point rubric may seem insufficient for some areas you wish to assess. This may be especially true when you are examining performance on a Project or other larger activity. A general five-level rubric follows:

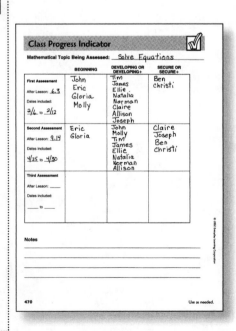

Sample Rubric

Beginning (B)
Students' responses have fragments of appropriate material and show effort to accomplish the task. Students do not explain either the concepts or procedures involved.

Developing (D)
Students accomplish part of the task independently. Students can partially explain the process but may need prompting to complete it.

Developing+ (D+)
Responses convince you that students can revise the work to a Secure performance with the help of feedback (for example, teacher prompts). While there is a basic understanding, it is not quite Secure or completely independent.

Secure (S)
Students' strategies and executions meet the demands of the task and demonstrate a firm grasp of the concepts and procedures involved. Their responses also demonstrate a broad range of understanding, and students apply their understanding in different contexts.

Secure+ (S+)
A Secure+ performance is exciting. In addition to meeting the qualifications for Secure, a student also merits distinction for special insights, good communication and reasoning, or other exceptional qualities.

Remember, the rubrics are only a framework. When you wish to use a rubric, the general indicators should be made more specific to fit the task, the time of year, and the grade level at which the rubric is being used. An example of a rubric applied to a specific task is illustrated in this book in the section on Class Progress Indicators beginning on page 24.

Finally, another example of a general rubric follows. This rubric might be applied to a problem in which students are asked both to find an answer and to explain (or illustrate) their reasoning.

Rubrics such as these can be used to assess not only individual performance but also group processes for problem-solving tasks.

Sample Rubric

Level 0
No attempts are made to solve the problem.

Level 1
Partial attempts are made. Reasoning is not explained. Problems are misunderstood or little progress is made.

Level 2
Students arrive at solutions, but solutions are incorrect. However, students clearly show reasoning and correct processes.
or:
Solutions are correct with little or no explanation given.

Level 3
Solutions are correct. Explanations are attempted but are incomplete.

Level 4
Solutions are correct. Explanations are clear and complete.

Level 5
Students give exemplary solutions.

Ongoing Assessment

Observing Students

Observing students during regular classroom interactions, as they work alone and in groups, is an important assessment technique in *Everyday Mathematics*. The methods described can help you manage ongoing observations. A discussion of record keeping follows.

Teacher-Guided Instruction

During the lesson, circulate around the room, interacting with the students and observing the mathematical behavior that is taking place. Identify those students who are having difficulty or showing progress. Be alert to significant comments and interactions. These quick observations often tell a great deal about a student's mathematical thinking. Practice making mental notes on the spot and follow them up with brief written notes when possible. The important thing is to find an efficient way to keep track of students' progress without getting overwhelmed with papers, lists, and notes.

Mathematical Mini-Interviews

Observing and listening to students as they work will enable you to note progress. However, there are times when brief verbal interactions with probing questions clarify and enhance observations. These brief, nonthreatening, one-on-one interactions, overheard by the rest of the class or conducted in private, encourage mathematical communication skills. They should apply to the content at hand during any instructional interaction.

Games

At the beginning of the year, when students are first becoming comfortable with *Everyday Mathematics* games, and while they are working in small groups, circulate around the classroom observing the strategies that students are employing. Once students are playing the games independently, use the time to work with a small group having difficulty. Use recording tools to note any valuable information regarding individual mathematical development. You can also use this time to conduct mathematical mini-interviews.

Mental Math and Reflexes

As you present the class with Mental Math and Reflexes situations, focus on a small group of students, perhaps five at a time. You should never feel that all students need to be observed every day.

Strategy Sharing

Over time, encourage each student to share his or her strategies while working at the board or overhead projector. It is during this time that you should assume the role of "guide on the side" rather than "sage on the stage." In the *Everyday Mathematics* classroom, many strategies are used; recording students' strategies will help you know how to address individual strengths and needs.

Slates

Periodically, record students' responses from their slate reviews. The *Teacher's Lesson Guide* offers suggested problems. You may begin with these problems or make up your own. Slate assessment offers both review and a quick assessment of students' progress toward computation mastery. You might focus on one group at a time and indicate only those students with Beginning understanding. Provide follow-up instruction for them based on your records.

Recording Observations

When observing students, you may use a number of recording tools to organize your observations. The following suggestions may be helpful to you. Choose one that appeals to you most and try it. If necessary, adapt it to make it more useful or try another tool.

Computer Labels

Print out students' names on sheets of large computer address labels. Write observations on the appropriate labels. As labels become filled, place them on numbered file cards and file them sequentially throughout the year.

Seating Charts or Calendar Grids

Place each student's name in a grid cell and write observations in the cells as you circulate throughout the classroom. After reflecting on whole-class needs, cut apart the cells, date them, and file them for each student. Or use self-stick notes in the cells. Replace full notes with new ones to avoid having to cut out cells. Use the notes to analyze individual strengths and needs and to prepare for parent conferences.

Class Checklists

A blank Class Checklist is provided in *Math Masters,* page 469. A mini version is shown on page 4 of this book. You may want to use it for recording ongoing observations and interactions by identifying a particular learning goal and using a rubric symbol to indicate students' progress on the checklist.

Product Assessment

Products from *Everyday Mathematics*

Samples of students' mathematical writings, drawings, and creations add balance to the assessment process. This section offers a review of some of the products that are part of *Everyday Mathematics,* as well as suggestions for outside sources for product assessment. Some of these items can be selected and stored in a portfolio or work folder along with other assessments.

Math Journals

Math Journals can be considered working portfolios. Students should keep the journals intact so that they can revisit, review, correct, and improve their responses at a later time. You and students might select journal pages focusing on topics of concern or story problems or those featuring open-ended tasks to photocopy and include in portfolios. You may access these pages to document students' progress on number collections, equivalent names for fractions, and scores on 50-facts tests. Two other types of journal pages that can be used as assessment are Math Boxes and Time to Reflect.

Math Boxes

Math Boxes are an important routine for reviewing and maintaining skills. They also offer an excellent opportunity for ongoing assessment, providing glimpses into how a student performs in several areas. References in the *Teacher's Lesson Guide* identify paired Math Boxes pages and tell which problems cover prerequisites for the next unit.

One method for record keeping when assessing work with Math Boxes is to circulate and make informal observations on a copy of the Math Boxes page. Record names and comments about individuals who are having difficulties on self-stick notes placed over individual Math Boxes.

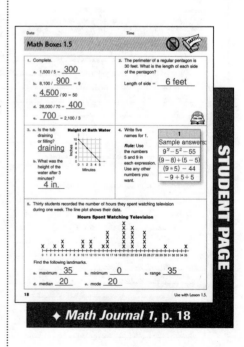

♦ *Math Journal 1,* p. 18

Time to Reflect

These self-assessment journal pages offer students an opportunity to reflect on their progress. These single-page activities include two or three open-ended questions that lead students to decide which concepts they are finding easy, difficult, or surprising. Students might be asked how they would teach a concept or skill. Some questions simply ask students to critique their own performance. Student responses on these pages can provide a useful insight into students' mathematical reasoning skills.

Additional Assessment Products

Many teachers are interested in gathering examples of students' writing and thinking in addition to those provided by *Everyday Mathematics* materials. This type of writing is usually more open-ended and allows teachers more flexibility in topics while they provide students with opportunities to reflect on, assess their understanding, and enhance their communication skills. This section provides examples of products you may wish to include in your assessment plan.

Math Logs

Some teachers find it beneficial for students to write about mathematics regularly. A spiral notebook or a set of log sheets can be used as a math log. (See sample masters in *Math Masters,* pages 472–474.) Not only can these written reflections serve as a powerful means of checking students' understanding, but they are also a means of assessing curiosity, persistence, risk taking, and self-confidence.

Remember that math logs are not "end products" but, instead, are an important part of the ongoing assessment process referred to in the introduction. They are helpful to both you and students only if they reveal useful feedback and encourage the development of mathematical thinking, understanding, and written communication.

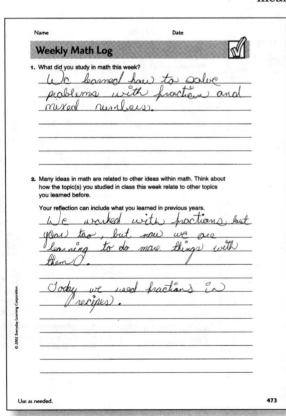

Here are some suggestions on how to encourage students to write:

Open-Ended Questions Use open-ended questions to start students writing. Some prompts that you can use are

• *What does the term* reciprocal *mean?*

• *What are relation symbols? Give examples of when you use them.*

• *Why is this answer right (wrong)? Explain.*

• *How do you know your answer is correct?*

• *What was your strategy for finding the solution?*

• *How many ways can you find a solution for this problem?*

• *Find the error in the following problem. Why is it an error?*

• *How is this like something you have learned before?*

Students may use Exit Slip sheets to record responses to open-ended questions at the close of a lesson or unit. (See *Math Masters,* page 478. A reduced version is shown on page 118 of this book.)

Number Stories Occasionally ask students to write a number story. Sometimes you may wish to supply the numbers. *For example:*

• *Write a number story that uses the numbers $\frac{2}{3}$ and 0.5.*

• *Write a number story that uses all square numbers less than 10.*

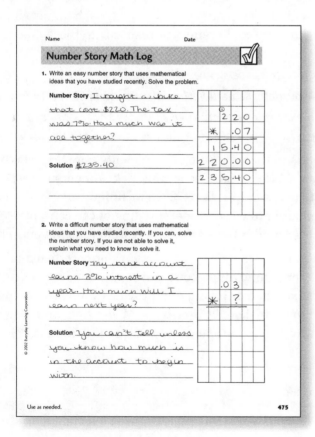

At other times, you may leave the instructions more open-ended:

- *Make up a number story using square units.*
- *Write a number story that uses a variable.*

Written number stories provide concrete assessment of students' understanding of operations, relationships, and numbers. For example, students might choose the incorrect operation to find an answer. Number stories often point out misconceptions.

Portfolio Writing If you are using portfolios, students can write entries for their portfolios. To help focus the writing, you might suggest that they write about one of the following topics:

- *What I Hope to Learn about Mathematics This Year*
- *Why Mathematics Is Important*
- *My Plan for Learning Mathematics*

As the year continues and entries change, ask students to update their introductions and tell why they have chosen the different pieces. At the end of the year, students could re-evaluate their portfolios and make a list of important concepts that they have learned.

Concept and Strategy Writing Prior to the teaching of a unit, invite students to share what they already know about the concepts being presented. For example, before you teach a unit on algebra concepts, students could reflect in response to these questions or topics:

- *What is a number sentence?*
- *How do you determine whether a number sentence is true or false?*
- *Write an example of a number sentence that is false. Then replace a variable with a number that will make the number sentence true.*

The answers to these questions/statements may help you plan your instruction. At the close of each unit, ask students to respond to the same statements or questions. This technique allows students and you to compare growth in understanding of the concepts. You may even discover a need to clear up some students' misconceptions.

Students can use words, representations, or both to explain their thinking. Communicating about mathematics encourages students to reflect upon their thinking and provides you with another window into their thought processes. Model this kind of writing on the overhead to show students how to use this format.

Alternatives to Math Logs

Even if you do not want to have students keep regular math logs, have them occasionally write about mathematics so they can develop their writing skills. During each unit, give students short writing assignments. Writing topics can be based on any of the math log suggestions given, or they can be short reflections written just before the end-of-unit assessment. *For example:*

• *The math I know best/least in this unit is _____.*

• *Uses for the mathematics I learned in this unit are _____.*

These assignments could also be more content-oriented. *For example:*

• *A CD that regularly costs $15 is on sale for 20% off. What is the discount in dollars?*

• *What is the sale price?*

Try to include students in the assessment process. The products listed below will encourage students to develop their ability to think reflectively. These products can be used as Math Messages or Math Boxes within the program or in math logs or alternatives to math logs.

Reflective Writing and Self-Assessment

Open-ended statements and questions, such as those suggested here, provide students with opportunities to reflect on what they know and what they do not know. Invite students to reflect before, during, and/or after a lesson. Here are some prompts you can use:

• *My goal for tomorrow is ...*

• *I learned that ...*

• *I was surprised that I ...*

• *I was pleased that I ...*

• *I still don't understand ...*

• *Because of the mathematics lesson today, I feel more confident about ...*

• *The most important thing I learned in* Everyday Mathematics *today (this week) is ...*

• *I think (percents, calculators) are ...*

• *(Multiplication) is easy if ...*

• *The trouble with mathematics is ...*

• *What I like most (or least) about Lesson X is ...*

• *How would you explain to an absent student what we did today?*

• *What was the most difficult (easiest) part of today's lesson?*

• *Write a test problem that I might give to see if you understand today's lesson.*

• *What did you learn today that you did not know before?*

• *What did you like or dislike about today's lesson? Why?*

NOTE: Do not feel discouraged if students have difficulty communicating mathematically. This is a skill that takes time to develop.

Students who begin the year having nothing to say or who answer in short, incomplete sentences become much more fluent as the year progresses.

How often should you use a math log or other writing in your math program? This depends on you and your students. While some teachers use logs a few times per week, you may find that once a week (perhaps on Friday, reflecting on what students did that week) or at the end of the unit is sufficient.

Choose the amount of additional writing with which you and your students feel comfortable.

Sometimes you may want students to focus on how they worked in a small group:

- *What worked well in your group today?*
- *Describe what your job was in your group today.*
- *What could you have done to help your group work better?*
- *What do you like or dislike about working in a group?*

End-of-Year Reflection This kind of writing may give teachers some ideas about students' attitudes toward mathematics and about which experiences have been the most beneficial. Responses will vary, depending on the writing ability and reflective experiences of the students.

End of Year Reflection

This year I learned how to do more with algebra. I learned how to use variables in Grades 4 and 5, but now I understand it better and it's more fun. It's like solving a puzzle. I even used it to solve some math problems at home.

I like to solve equations with variables, especially the problems that deal with real life. We need math to do many things, and that's why I like math.

Periodic Assessment

Periodic assessment activities are those that are done at fairly consistent times or intervals over the school year. This section briefly reviews periodic assessment sources that are currently part of *Everyday Mathematics* and then discusses additional sources that experienced teachers use.

Sources from *Everyday Mathematics*

Unit Reviews and Assessments

Each unit of your *Teacher's Lesson Guide* ends with a review and assessment lesson that lists the learning goals for that unit. The goals list is followed by a cumulative review that includes suggestions for oral and slate assessments as well as group or independent written assessment ideas and performance assessment activities. Assessment lessons also include a self-assessment page called "Time to Reflect" in students' journals.

This cumulative oral, slate, and written review provides an opportunity for you to check students' progress on concepts and skills that were introduced or further developed in the unit. In addition to these resources, here are other suggestions:

- Use rubrics to record progress toward each learning goal you assess. Rubrics are introduced on pages 13 and 14 of this book, and examples of how to use them are provided on pages 24–26 and in the unit Assessment Overviews section beginning on page 37.

- Only a few of the concepts and skills from any unit are suggested for assessment at the end of each unit. Feel free to add items that you believe need assessing. You may also wish to delete items with which students are Secure.

- Since many of the end-of-unit reviews and assessments tend to focus on skills, you may want to add more concept-oriented and open-ended questions as suggested in the Product Assessment section of this book, beginning on page 17.

- Accumulate information from the skills lists (in the review and assessment lessons) and then add them to the Quarterly Class Checklists and Individual Profiles of Progress.

Assessing Students' Journal Work

You might use rubrics to periodically assess pages within journals as independent reviews. Also, several activities throughout the journals have students glue their best work onto the page. You might develop a rubric to assess these activities as well. By recording your individual objectives on a Class Progress Indicator or a Class Checklist, you can ascertain which students may need additional experience. These students can then be paired with students who are proficient in that particular skill or activity.

Midyear and End-of-Year Assessments

The Midyear and End-of-Year Assessment Masters (*Math Masters*, pages 420–433) provide additional assessment opportunities that you may wish to use as part of your balanced assessment plan. Minis of these masters, with answers, are shown on pages 89–96 of this book. These tests cover important concepts and skills presented in Sixth Grade *Everyday Mathematics*, but they are not designed to be used as "pretests," and they should not be your primary assessment tools. Use them along with the ongoing, product, and periodic assessments that are found within the lessons and at the end of each unit.

Additional Sources for Periodic Assessment

Class Progress Indicators

Class Progress Indicators, also known as Performance Charts, are another assessment tool that some teachers have found useful in assessing and tracking students' progress on selected mathematical topics.

A Class Progress Indicator form provides space to record students' performance on any mathematical topic you choose to assess two or three times during the year.

The first assessment opportunity, which usually occurs after students have some exposure to and experience with a topic, provides a baseline for your students' performance early in the year. By recording the second and third assessments on the same form, you can track the progress of each student as well as the whole class throughout the school year. A sixth grade teacher's sample Class Progress Indicator is shown on page 25. A blank form of this master is provided in *Math Masters*, page 470.

© 2002 Everyday Learning Corporation

Class Progress Indicator

Mathematical Topic Being Assessed: Solve Equations

	BEGINNING	DEVELOPING OR DEVELOPING+	SECURE OR SECURE+
First Assessment After Lesson: 6.3 Dates included: 2/6 to 2/12	John Eric Gloria Molly	Tim James Ellie Natalia Norman Claire Allison Joseph	Ben Christi
Second Assessment After Lesson: 9.14 Dates included: 4/25 to 4/30	Eric Gloria	John Molly Tim James Ellie Natalia Norman Allison	Claire Joseph Ben Christi
Third Assessment After Lesson: _____ Dates included: _____ to _____			

Notes

_____

_____

_____

_____

470

Use as needed.

Record the names of students under the columns that best indicate their ability levels: Beginning, Developing, or Secure, or whatever rubric symbols you like to use. If you wish, use (+) to indicate students who are between these levels. As you conduct your assessments, keep this question in mind: What do I need to do instructionally to promote progress? Space is provided at the bottom of the form for any notes you may wish to make.

Below is an example of a mathematical topic and an accompanying rubric.

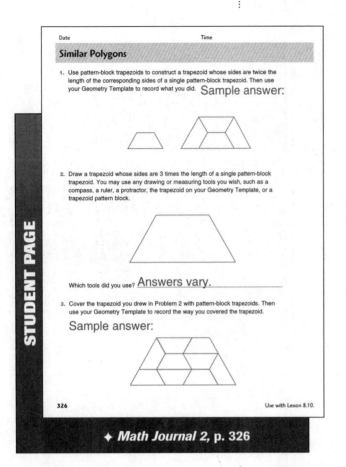

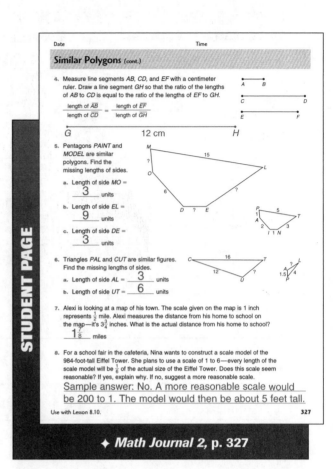

Sample Similar Polygons Rubric

Beginning (B)
Drawings show some sides with correct dimensions but may appear lopsided. Students use a variety of tools in a trial-and-error methodology.

Developing (D)
Drawings display correct proportions. Students may need help from a partner in deciding which tools to use.

Secure (S)
Drawings display correct proportions. Students choose tools and draw the trapezoids on their own. Students may help others in the classroom. Students use tools efficiently.

Remember, the more experience you have with the range of students' responses, the easier it will be to determine or assign rubrics.

Class Checklists and Individual Profiles of Progress

To help you keep track of students' progress in areas that are important to your school and district, the authors of *Everyday Mathematics* have provided learning goals checklists for individuals and for the class. These Class Checklists and Individual Profiles of Progress are provided for each unit as well as for each quarter. They are found at the back of your *Math Masters* book on pages 434–466 and are reproduced in a reduced version in the Assessment Masters section of this book on pages 96–112.

The checklists identify learning outcomes for each unit of *Everyday Mathematics* and indicate the approximate level of proficiency expected: *Beginning, Developing,* or *Secure.* For many of the learning goals, the level is identified as "Developing" rather than "Secure." "Developing" topics have been included so that you can record student progress over time.

Many of these learning goals are assessed at the end of each unit; all of them are developed on journal pages. You may want to use the checklists to help you give priorities to lesson materials.

The checklists assume that students had *Everyday Mathematics* in earlier grades. You may need to make adjustments for students who used other mathematics programs.

First, use the Class Checklists to gather and record information. Then, transfer selected information to the Individual Profiles of Progress sheet for each student's portfolio or for use during parent conferences.

The information recorded on the checklists can be obtained from end-of-unit oral and written assessments. In fact, you may want to bypass the Class Checklists and record this information from these assessments directly onto the Individual Profiles of Progress.

◆ **Math Masters, p. 442**

◆ **Math Masters, p. 443**

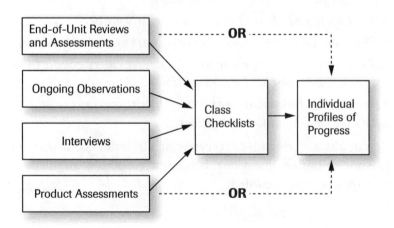

Blank profile and checklist masters can be found in *Math Masters,* pages 468 and 469. You may wish to record information from other sources, such as journal review pages, Math Boxes, Math Messages, and math logs.

Information obtained from teacher-directed instruction is also a good resource to be recorded on the Class Checklists or directly on Individual Profiles of Progress. As mentioned in the Ongoing Assessment section of this book, information can also be obtained from observations, questions, and other sources during regular instructional interactions.

Individual Mathematical Interviews

Periodic interviews of ten to fifteen minutes with each student are a splendid idea and will prove valuable and revealing. They are, however, very difficult to carry out, given the full classroom schedule and the need to provide supervision for the rest of the class.

A compromise would be at least one goal-oriented, five-minute talk with each student during the year. At the start of the year, the interview might focus on the student's preparation for the content to come. At midyear, the interview might be concerned with how the work in mathematics has been going. Near the year's end, it might involve the student's preparation for next year.

The interview can be conducted while the rest of the class is playing mathematical games or working independently. Teachers have also suggested if it is feasible, to make "appointments" to have lunch with students individually or with two or three students at a time. Other appointments might be arranged before class begins, during recess, or after school.

The following are suggested questions for a midyear interview:
• *How do you feel about mathematics?*
• *What have you enjoyed most about mathematics?*
• *What has been the easiest (hardest) part of mathematics for you?*
• *How can we work together to help you feel more comfortable with these difficult parts of mathematics?*
• *How do you feel about working with partners and in small groups for some mathematics activities?*

You might also consider interviewing students about their responses to Time to Reflect questions. Students' responses might be recorded on paper or tape-recorded.

"My Math Class" Inventories

At the beginning of the year, you may want students to complete an inventory to assess their mathematical attitudes. This inventory might be repeated later in the year to see whether their attitudes have changed. Two samples (Evaluating My Math Class; My Math Class) are shown below. Blank masters of these inventories are found in *Math Masters,* pages 471 and 472. Inventories can be included in students' portfolios and discussed during individual interviews or parent conferences.

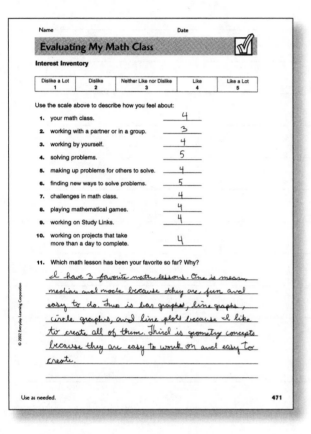

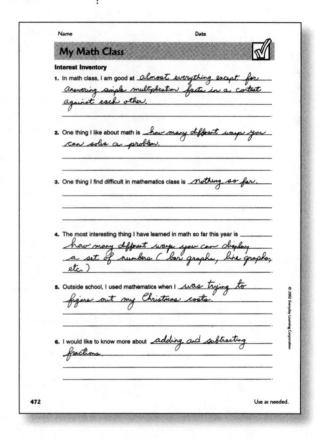

Your Assessment Ideas

_____
_____
_____
_____
_____
_____
_____
_____
_____
_____
_____
_____
_____
_____
_____
_____
_____
_____
_____
_____
_____
_____
_____
_____
_____
_____

Your Assessment Ideas

Grading

Traditionally, the main purpose of end-of-unit assessments is to help the teacher monitor student progress and evaluate student achievement. In addition, end-of-unit assessments in *Everyday Mathematics* provide valuable information for planning future lessons.

The philosophy behind the end-of-unit assessments agrees with that expressed in the NCTM *Assessment Standards for School Mathematics* (1995). The diagram below, which is taken from that publication, illustrates how the four purposes of assessment translate into classroom practices:

Four Purposes of Assessment and Their Results

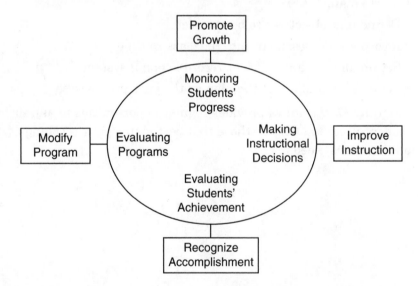

Because *Everyday Mathematics* presents concepts and skills repeatedly throughout the year, it is important to know how students are progressing individually on a concept or skill, as well as how much the class as a whole understands it. For that reason, the end-of-unit assessments in *Everyday Mathematics* include items at an exposure step of the spiral, in addition to items that assess mastery.

On the basis of students' performance on these assessment tools, teachers can make informed decisions about how to approach concepts and skills in future lessons. For example, several students may correctly answer a question on fraction addition, but the class as a whole is not Secure at it. The teacher knows that the next time the skill appears in the spiral, he or she can call on student leaders to help get the class started.

Since end-of-unit assessments have several purposes, they should not be the only source for grades. Following are some of the ways to accumulate scores for student grades:

- Create open-ended problems or use those that are in the journal. Grade the answers to these problems according to a rubric that assigns points to the different performance levels.
- Record scores on cumulative reviews.
- Record scores on review masters.
- Develop interim quizzes.
- Assign points for successful group problem solving.
- Weigh the value of questions on the end-of-unit assessments, checking progress according to your expectations for mastery.

This list is only a beginning. Assessment is as individual as are teaching styles. While developing your own assessment plan for *Everyday Mathematics,* consider the following guidelines:

- Start small.
- Define unit objectives to be assessed.
- Incorporate assessment into the class routine.
- Set up an easy and efficient record-keeping system.
- Personalize and adapt the plan as the year progresses.

Everyday Mathematics provides regular opportunities to assess student progress. Choose those that best match your teaching style and students' needs.

Outside Tests

Outside tests are generally tests given at the school, district, or state level, or they are nationally standardized tests. Most teachers are familiar with the standardized tests that have multiple-choice responses. The frustrating aspect of this type of test is that it analyzes a narrow range of mathematical thinking and doesn't assess the depth and breadth of the mathematical knowledge that should be attained in a well-implemented *Everyday Mathematics* classroom.

There are ways to help your students function well in testing environments. Math Boxes, for example, can be tailored to help prepare students for the formats of an outside test. Even without such preparation, *Everyday Mathematics* students generally do about as well on the computation sections of standardized tests and much better on concepts and problem-solving sections, as students in traditional programs.

More recently, performance assessments or open-ended tests have been developed. These tests report results similar to those from traditional tests—class and individual norms (percentile rankings)—but they also attempt to test problem solving and communication skills on larger tasks. Some of these tests provide rubric scores along with normed data. Try to encourage the use of one of these newer performance-based tests at the district level rather than the traditional multiple-choice tests.

Performance-based assessments developed at the school or district level probably afford the best opportunity to reflect the instructional practices in local classrooms. Teams of teachers and administrators can develop assessments and rubrics that enhance the learning process rather than focus on narrow thinking used only in a small portion of mathematical activities. At some grade levels, these assessments can be used exclusively. When standardized testing is mandatory at a certain grade level, these assessments can give a better picture of the mathematical education occurring in the classroom.

Your Assessment Ideas

Your Assessment Ideas

Recommended Reading

Black, Paul, and Dylan Wiliam. "Assessment and Classroom Learning." *Assessment in Education* (March 1998): 7–74.

———. "Inside the Black Box: Raising Standards Through Classroom Assessment." *Phi Delta Kappan* 80, no. 2 (October 1998): 139–149.

Bryant, Brian R., and Teddy Maddox. "Using Alternative Assessment Techniques to Plan and Evaluate Mathematics." *LD Forum* 21, no. 2 (winter 1996): 24–33.

Eisner, Elliot W. "The Uses and Limits of Performance Assessment." *Phi Delta Kappan* 80, no. 9 (May 1999): 658–661.

Kuhn, Gerald. *Mathematics Assessment: What Works in the Classroom.* San Francisco: Jossey-Bass Publishers, 1994.

National Council of Teachers of Mathematics (NCTM). *Curriculum and Evaluation Standards for School Mathematics.* Reston, Va.: NCTM, 1989.

———. *Assessment Standards for School Mathematics.* Reston, Va.: NCTM, 1995.

———. *Principles and Standards for School Mathematics.* Reston, Va.: NCTM, 2000.

National Research Council, Mathematical Sciences Education Board. *Measuring What Counts: A Conceptual Guide for Mathematics Assessment.* Washington, D.C.: National Academy Press, 1993.

Pearson, Bethyl, and Cathy Berghoff. "London Bridge Is Not Falling Down: It's Supporting Alternative Assessment." *TESOL Journal* 5, no. 4 (summer 1996): 28–31.

Shepard, Lorrie A. "Using Assessment to Improve Learning." *Educational Leadership* 52, no. 5 (February 1995): 38–43.

Stenmark, Jean Kerr, ed. *Mathematics Assessment: Myths, Models, Good Questions, and Practical Suggestions.* Reston, Va.: National Council of Teachers of Mathematics, 1991.

Stiggens, Richard J. *Student-Centered Classroom Assessment.* Englewood Cliffs, N.J.: Prentice-Hall, 1997.

Webb, N. L., and A. F. Coxford, eds. *Assessment in the Mathematics Classroom: 1993 Yearbook.* Reston, Va.: National Council of Teachers of Mathematics, 1993.

Your Assessment Ideas

_____

_____

_____

_____

_____

_____

_____

_____

_____

_____

_____

_____

_____

_____

_____

_____

_____

_____

_____

_____

_____

_____

_____

_____

Your Assessment Ideas

Assessment Overviews

This section offers examples of how to use different types of assessments in specific lessons. For each unit, you will find examples of three major types of assessment opportunities: Ongoing Assessment, Product Assessment, and Periodic Assessment. Keep in mind, however, that these are not distinct categories; they frequently overlap. For example, some Periodic Assessments may also serve as Product Assessments that you or the student may choose to keep in the student's portfolio.

Contents   **Page**

Unit 1
Assessment Overview

There are many pathways to a balanced assessment plan. As you teach Unit 1, start to become familiar with some of the approaches to assessment. The next few pages provide examples of the three major types of assessment suggested in this program: Ongoing Assessment, Product Assessment, and Periodic Assessment. This assessment overview offers examples of ways to assess students on what they learn in Unit 1. Do not try to use all of the examples, but begin with a few that meet your needs.

Ongoing Assessment Opportunities

Ongoing assessment provides opportunities to observe students during regular interactions as they work independently and in groups. You can conduct ongoing assessment during teacher-guided instruction, Math Boxes sessions, mathematical mini-interviews, games, Mental Math and Reflexes sessions, strategy sharing, and slate work. The chart below provides a summary of ongoing assessment opportunities in Unit 1 as they relate to specific Unit 1 learning goals.

1e **Secure Goal** Identify landmarks of data sets. (Lessons 1.2–1.5, 1.9, and 1.11)	Lesson 1.2, p. 23 Lesson 1.3, p. 26 Lesson 1.5, p. 36
1f **Secure Goal** Compute and understand the mean. (Lessons 1.3–1.5, 1.9, and 1.11)	Lesson 1.3, p. 26 Lesson 1.5, p. 36

Product Assessment Opportunities

Math Journals, Math Boxes, Activity Sheets, *Math Masters,* math logs, and the results of Projects all provide product assessment opportunities. Here is an example of how you might use a rubric to assess students' ability to read graphs.

ALTERNATIVE ASSESSMENT **Report on Collected Graphs**

Students use what they know about graphs to assemble a report on the graphs they have collected from news magazines and newspapers. The sample rubric below can help you evaluate students' understanding of graphs.

Portfolio
Ideas

Sample Rubric

Beginning (B)
The student collects a graph in order to create a report. He or she attempts to fill out *Math Masters,* page 17 but experiences difficulty with some of the questions, such as drawing a reasonable conclusion or making a reasonable prediction based on the graph. As a result, teacher assistance is required. The student does not "write" a report beyond filling out *Math Masters,* page 17 and does not create a different graph to display the same type of data.

Developing (D)
The student collects a graph to create a report. He or she completes the questions on *Math Masters,* page 17 with little or no teacher assistance. By completing *Math Masters,* page 17, the student summarizes and describes data appropriately from the graph and is able to generate a question related to the data. He or she makes reasonable predictions and draws appropriate conclusions. The student may also find inaccurate or unfair mathematics in relationship to the display or scale used. The student attempts to create a different graph using the same data, but teacher guidance is required.

Secure (S)
The student creates a report based on the graph(s) he or she collected. Without teacher assistance, *Math Masters,* page 17 is completed correctly, and the information is used to create a report. The report includes inferences made by interpreting the graph appropriately and makes generalizations that are communicated clearly and logically. He or she creates an alternative display (graph), using the same data. The student may complete more than one report, which may be assembled into an individual booklet of graphs.

Periodic Assessment Opportunities

Here is a summary of the periodic assessment opportunities that are provided in Unit 1. Refer to Lesson 1.12 for details.

Oral and Slate Assessment

In Lesson 1.12, you will find oral and slate assessment problems on pages 68 and 69.

Written Assessment

In Lesson 1.12, you will find written assessment problems on pages 69 and 70 (*Math Masters,* pages 387–390).

See the following chart to find oral, slate, and written assessment problems that address specific learning goals.

1a	**Beginning Goal** Interpret and construct step graphs. (Lesson 1.7)	Written Assessment, Problems 15–19
1b	**Developing Goal** Interpret mystery graphs. (Lessons 1.2–1.4)	Written Assessment, Problem 1
1c	**Developing/Secure Goal** Use a Percent Circle to interpret circle graphs. (Lessons 1.8 and 1.11)	Written Assessment, Problem 4
1d	**Secure Goal** Find equivalent names for numbers. (Lesson 1.3)	Slate Assessment, Problems 1 and 2
1e	**Secure Goal** Identify landmarks of data sets. (Lessons 1.2–1.5, 1.9, and 1.11)	Oral Assessment, Problem 1 Written Assessment, Problems 2 and 11–13
1f	**Secure Goal** Compute and understand the mean. (Lessons 1.3–1.5, 1.9, and 1.11)	Oral Assessment, Problem 1 Written Assessment, Problems 3 and 9
1g	**Secure Goal** Interpret and construct broken-line graphs. (Lessons 1.5, 1.6, 1.9, and 1.10)	Written Assessment, Problems 5–8
1h	**Secure Goal** Interpret and construct bar graphs. (Lessons 1.6 and 1.11)	Written Assessment, Problems 10–14

Alternative Assessment

In Lesson 1.12, you will find an alternative assessment option on page 70.

+ **Report on Collected Graphs**

Use the suggestions and rubric on page 39 to assess students' understanding of graphs by having them report on graphs they have collected from news magazines and newspapers.

TEACHING MASTER

Name _____ Date _____ Time _____

Reading a Graph

Fill out this form for each graph you collect. Answers vary.

1. Title of graph _____
2. Source _____
3. Purpose of graph _____
4. Is the graph attractive? _____ Is it easy to read? _____
5. Does the graph appear to be fair and accurate? _____
6. What revision(s) would improve the graph? _____

7. Can you draw a conclusion from or make a prediction based on this graph? _____
   If so, what? _____

8. What is one question that a classmate could answer by reading the graph?
   _____

Challenge

9. A particular type of graph was selected to display the data. Sketch a different type of graph that could display the same data.

Use with Lesson 1.12.   17

+ *Math Masters*, p. 17

Unit 2
Assessment Overview

If you tried some of the assessment approaches that were suggested in the Unit 1 Assessment Overview, you are probably beginning to appreciate how the goal charts in this section can help you plan your assessment strategies. For example, at this point students are expected to be at a Secure level for adding and subtracting decimals (see Goal 2j in the chart below). The chart alerts you to the fact that ongoing assessment opportunities related to that goal are provided in Lessons 2.1 and 2.8 on pages 87 and 119 of your *Teacher's Lesson Guide*. In similar fashion, you can use the chart on page 43 to find written assessment opportunities related to this same goal.

Ongoing Assessment Opportunities

Ongoing assessment provides opportunities to observe students during regular interactions as they work independently and in groups. You can conduct ongoing assessment during teacher-guided instruction, Math Boxes sessions, mathematical mini-interviews, games, Mental Math and Reflexes sessions, strategy sharing, and slate work. The chart below provides a summary of ongoing assessment opportunities in Unit 2 as they relate to specific Unit 2 learning goals.

2b **Developing Goal** Estimate products and multiply decimals. (Lessons 2.2–2.4)	Lesson 2.2, p. 93 Lesson 2.4, p. 102 Lesson 2.8, p. 119
2h **Secure Goal** Use exponential notation for large numbers. (Lessons 2.7 and 2.8)	Lesson 2.7, p. 114
2j **Secure Goal** Add and subtract decimals. (Lesson 2.1)	Lesson 2.1, p. 87 Lesson 2.8, p. 119
2k **Secure Goal** Estimate quotients and divide whole numbers. (Lesson 2.10)	Lesson 2.10, pp. 127 and 129

Product Assessment Opportunities

Math Journals, Math Boxes, Activity Sheets, *Math Masters,* math logs, and the results of Projects all provide product assessment opportunities. Here is an example of how you might use a rubric to assess students' ability to describe a decimal computation strategy.

Lesson 2.12, p. 140

ALTERNATIVE ASSESSMENT **Describe a Decimal Computation Strategy**

Understanding how to insert decimal points in answers is an essential part of addition, subtraction, multiplication, or division with decimals. This activity gives students an opportunity to apply their understanding of decimal computation by solving problems and then describing the strategies they used. Use your own rubric or the sample rubric below to evaluate students' work.

Sample Rubric

Beginning (B)
The student requires teacher assistance in solving the decimal computation problem. The student is still building an understanding of the decimal computation strategy that he or she is using for addition, subtraction, multiplication, and division. As a result, the correct answer is not given and the work provided is not understandable. The student will attempt to describe the strategy used but, due to lack of decimal computation understanding, he or she cannot explain the strategy adequately.

Developing (D)
The student attempts to solve the decimal computation problem but some teacher assistance may be required to complete the problem. He or she demonstrates partial or satisfactory understanding of decimal computation. As a result, the answer may not be correct. The student attempts to articulate his or her strategy by using appropriate terminology, but some teacher assistance may be required to get started.

Secure (S)
The student solves the decimal computation problem independently. He or she displays a strong understanding of decimal computation and, as a result, has a correct solution. He or she clearly and effectively describes the strategy used.

Periodic Assessment Opportunities

Here is a summary of the periodic assessment opportunities that are provided in Unit 2. Refer to Lesson 2.12 for details.

Oral and Slate Assessment

In Lesson 2.12, you will find oral and slate assessment problems on pages 138 and 139.

Written Assessment

In Lesson 2.12, you will find written assessment problems on pages 139 and 140 (*Math Masters,* pages 391–393).

See the following chart to find oral, slate, and written assessment problems that address specific learning goals.

2a	**Beginning Goal** Translate between scientific notation and standard notation, with and without a calculator. (Lessons 2.8 and 2.9)	Oral Assessment, Problems 3 and 4 Slate Assessment, Problems 5 and 6 Written Assessment, Problems 4 and 5
2b	**Developing Goal** Estimate products and multiply decimals. (Lessons 2.2–2.4)	Slate Assessment, Problem 3 Written Assessment, Problems 22–25
2c	**Developing Goal** Divide two whole numbers; give the answer to a specified number of decimal places. (Lessons 2.10 and 2.11)	Slate Assessment, Problem 3 Written Assessment, Problem 31
2d	**Developing Goal** Estimate the quotient and divide a decimal by a whole number. (Lesson 2.11)	Slate Assessment, Problem 3 Written Assessment, Problems 29 and 30
2e	**Developing Goal** Multiply by positive and negative powers of 10. (Lesson 2.4)	Slate Assessment, Problem 4
2f	**Developing Goal** Interpret number-and-word notation for large numbers. (Lesson 2.5)	Written Assessment, Problems 3, 5, and 7–10
2g	**Developing Goal** Use exponential notation for small numbers. (Lesson 2.6)	Written Assessment, Problems 12, 14, and 15
2h	**Secure Goal** Use exponential notation for large numbers. (Lessons 2.7 and 2.8)	Oral Assessment, Problem 3 Slate Assessment, Problem 5 Written Assessment, Problems 11, 13, 16, and 17
2i	**Developing/Secure Goal** Read, write, and compare numbers from thousandths to trillions. (Lessons 2.5–2.9)	Oral Assessment, Problems 1–4 Slate Assessment, Problems 1, 2, and 5 Written Assessment, Problems 1–6
2j	**Secure Goal** Add and subtract decimals. (Lesson 2.1)	Written Assessment, Problems 18–21
2k	**Secure Goal** Estimate quotients and divide whole numbers. (Lesson 2.10)	Written Assessment, Problems 26–28 and 31

Alternative Assessment

In Lesson 2.12, you will find an alternative assessment option on page 140.

✦ Describe a Decimal Computation Strategy

Use the suggestions and rubric on page 42 to assess students' ability to solve decimal computation problems.

✦ **Math Masters, p. 436**

Unit 3
Assessment Overview

At this stage in their learning, most of your sixth grade students should be either at a Secure level or still Developing many of the pre-algebra learning goals in this unit. One aim of this unit is to prepare students for the fractions in Unit 4. The chart below indicates that there are two ongoing assessment opportunities related to goals 3h and 3i, which are skills you need for computing with fractions. They can be found in Lessons 3.7 and 3.10 on pages 185 and 199 of your *Teacher's Lesson Guide.* Similarly, the chart on page 46 indicates where you can find slate assessment problems to gauge students' progress toward these same goals.

Ongoing Assessment Opportunities

Ongoing assessment provides opportunities to observe students during regular interactions as they work independently and in groups. You can conduct ongoing assessment during teacher-guided instruction, Math Boxes sessions, mathematical mini-interviews, games, Mental Math and Reflexes sessions, strategy sharing, and slate work. The chart below provides a summary of ongoing assessment opportunities in Unit 3 as they relate to specific Unit 3 learning goals.

3h **Secure Goal** Convert between fractions and mixed numbers. (Lessons 3.1–3.4)	Lesson 3.7, p. 185 Lesson 3.10, p. 199
3i **Secure Goal** Find the least common multiple of two numbers. (Lessons 3.5 and 3.6)	Lesson 3.7, p. 185 Lesson 3.10, p. 199

Product Assessment Opportunities

Math Journals, Math Boxes, Activity Sheets, *Math Masters,* math logs, and the results of Projects all provide product assessment opportunities. Here is an example of how you might use a rubric to assess students' ability to make graphs.

Lesson 3.9, p. 195

ENRICHMENT **Constructing Mystery Graphs**

This activity is a good way to assess students'
understanding and ability to create mystery graphs.
Use your own rubric, or the sample rubric below, to
evaluate students' work.

Sample Rubric
Beginning (B)
The student attempts to create a mystery graph but may require some assistance deciding on a situation that would be appropriate OR the situation selected may not be appropriate for mystery graphs. The student creates a graph on the grid but errors are made and the horizontal and vertical axes are not labeled. As a result, the student has difficulty describing the situation that corresponds to the graph.
Developing (D)
The student creates a mystery graph independently, using an appropriate topic or situation. Some minor errors may need correcting. The horizontal and vertical axes are labeled. The student may require some assistance, however, in describing the situation that corresponds to the graph.
Secure (S)
The student independently creates a mystery graph, using an appropriate topic or situation. The horizontal and vertical axes are labeled correctly. The description of the situation is communicated, clearly showing a direct correlation with the graph.

Periodic Assessment Opportunities

Here is a summary of the periodic assessment opportunities that
are provided in Unit 3. Refer to Lesson 3.11 for details.

Oral and Slate Assessment

In Lesson 3.11, you will find oral and slate assessment problems on
pages 202 and 203.

Written Assessment

In Lesson 3.11, you will find written assessment problems on
page 204 (*Math Masters,* pages 394–396).

See the chart below to find oral, slate, and written assessment
problems that address specific learning goals.

3a	**Beginning Goal** Use variables to describe general patterns. (Lessons 3.1 and 3.2)	Written Assessment, Problems 1 and 2
3b	**Developing Goal** Use a spreadsheet. (Lessons 3.7 and 3.8)	Written Assessment, Problems 6–9
3c	**Developing/Secure Goal** Interpret mystery graphs. (Lesson 3.9)	Written Assessment, Problem 17
3d	**Developing Goal** Write algebraic expressions to represent situations. (Lessons 3.3 and 3.9)	Oral Assessment, Problem 1 Slate Assessment, Problem 1 Written Assessment, Problems 3–5 and 11

3e **Developing Goal** Evaluate algebraic expressions and formulas. (Lessons 3.3–3.5, 3.7, and 3.8)	Slate Assessment, Problem 1 Written Assessment, Problems 9, 10, and 12–15
3f **Secure Goal** Mentally add 1-digit integers. (Lessons 3.7, 3.8, and 3.10)	Slate Assessment, Problem 4
3g **Secure Goal** Represent rates with formulas, tables, and graphs. (Lessons 3.5, 3.9, and 3.10)	Written Assessment, Problem 16
3h **Secure Goal** Convert between fractions and mixed numbers. (Lessons 3.1–3.4)	Slate Assessment, Problems 2 and 3
3i **Secure Goal** Find the least common multiple of two numbers. (Lessons 3.5 and 3.6)	Slate Assessment, Problem 5
3j **Secure Goal** Find the greatest common factor of two numbers. (Lessons 3.7 and 3.8)	Slate Assessment, Problem 6

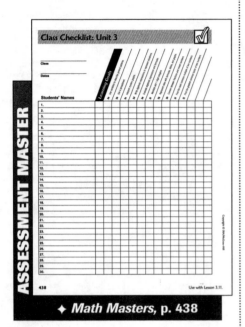

ASSESSMENT MASTER

◆ Math Masters, p. 438

Alternative Assessment

In Lesson 3.11, you will find alternative assessment options on page 204.

✦ Evaluate Formulas

This activity can help you assess students' ability to use a formula, as well as their problem-solving skills. Students use a formula to decide how much a fund-raiser can earn. You might consider using the rubric on page 45 to evaluate students' abilities, or, alternatively, use questions such as the following:

- Does the student substitute correctly in the formula?
- Once the student substitutes in the formula, can the student simplify it correctly?
- Can the student use the result to answer the question that is posed?

✦ Interpret Mystery Graphs

In this activity, students interpret graphs and tell a story from a graph. As you observe students playing the game, use a Class Checklist or calendar grids to record students' progress. Keep the following questions in mind:

- Does the student recognize that when the graph is horizontal, it means that the distance doesn't change; in other words, that the object is at rest?
- Does the student realize that the steeper the slope of the graph, the faster the object is moving?
- Does the student's story fit the graph?

Unit 4
Assessment Overview

In this unit, students further develop their ability to work with fractions. Depending on the specific skill, students' ability levels might range from Developing to Secure. A good mix of ongoing assessment opportunities is suggested in the chart below for all the learning goals that deal with fractions. Periodic assessments for these same goals are listed in the chart on page 49.

Ongoing Assessment Opportunities

Ongoing assessment provides opportunities to observe students during regular interactions as they work independently and in groups. You can conduct ongoing assessment during teacher-guided instruction, Math Boxes sessions, mathematical mini-interviews, games, Mental Math and Reflexes sessions, strategy sharing, and slate work. The chart below provides a summary of ongoing assessment opportunities in Unit 4 as they relate to specific Unit 4 learning goals.

4a **Developing Goal** Construct circle graphs with the Percent Circle. (Lessons 4.10 and 4.11)	Lesson 4.10, p. 265
4b **Developing Goal** Use an algorithm to multiply fractions and mixed numbers. (Lessons 4.6 and 4.7)	Lesson 4.7, p. 250
4c **Developing Goal** Use an algorithm to add and subtract mixed numbers having fractions with unlike denominators. (Lesson 4.5)	Lesson 4.5, p. 242 Lesson 4.8, p. 255
4d **Developing Goal** Use an algorithm to subtract mixed numbers having fractions with like denominators. (Lesson 4.4)	Lesson 4.4, p. 238 Lesson 4.8, p. 255
4e **Developing Goal** Find a percent of a number. (Lesson 4.11)	Lesson 4.11, p. 269
4f **Secure Goal** Use an algorithm to add mixed numbers having fractions with like denominators. (Lesson 4.4)	Lesson 4.4, p. 238 Lesson 4.8, p. 255
4g **Secure Goal** Use an algorithm to add and subtract fractions with like and unlike denominators. (Lesson 4.3)	Lesson 4.3, p. 231 Lesson 4.8, p. 255
4i **Secure Goal** Convert between fractions, mixed numbers, decimals, and percents. (Lessons 4.1, 4.3–4.5, and 4.7–4.9)	Lesson 4.1, pp. 221 and 222
4j **Secure Goal** Write fractions and mixed numbers in simplest form. (Lessons 4.1 and 4.4)	Lesson 4.8, p. 255

Product Assessment Opportunities

Math Journals, Math Boxes, Activity Sheets, *Math Masters,* math logs, and the results of Projects all provide product assessment opportunities. Here is an example of how you might use a rubric to assess students' ability to write and solve fraction number stories.

Lesson 4.12, p. 277

ALTERNATIVE ASSESSMENT **Write and Solve Fraction Number Stories**

A good way to assess students' understanding of fraction computation is to have students write fraction number stories. Use your own rubric, or the sample rubric below, to evaluate students' work.

Portfolio
Ideas

Sample Rubric

Beginning (B)
The student attempts to write a fraction number story but has difficulty displaying an understanding of the fraction operation (addition, subtraction, or multiplication) being used. As a result, teacher assistance is required. Unrelated data may be included, or data that is needed may be missing. Many of the required components of the story are missing, such as the story, number sentence, unit, question, and possibly a picture or diagram, if appropriate.

Developing (D)
The student attempts to write a fraction number story independently but may require some assistance or prompting in order to get started. He or she displays an understanding of the fraction operation selected and includes most of the necessary components, such as the story, number sentence, unit, question, and possibly a picture or diagram, if appropriate.

Secure (S)
The student writes a fraction number story independently, displaying a clear understanding of the fraction operation selected. The student may intentionally include additional data in the story. All the components of a number story are included, such as story, number sentence, unit, question, and a picture or diagram, if appropriate.

Periodic Assessment Opportunities

Here is a summary of the periodic assessment opportunities that are provided in Unit 4. Refer to Lesson 4.12 for details.

Oral and Slate Assessment

In Lesson 4.12, you will find oral and slate assessment problems on pages 273–275.

Written Assessment

In Lesson 4.12, you will find written assessment problems on page 275 (*Math Masters,* pages 397–399).

See the following chart to find oral, slate, and written assessment problems that address specific learning goals.

4a	**Developing Goal** Construct circle graphs with the Percent Circle. (Lessons 4.10 and 4.11)	Written Assessment, Problem 40
4b	**Developing Goal** Use an algorithm to multiply fractions and mixed numbers. (Lessons 4.6 and 4.7)	Oral Assessment, Problem 2 Written Assessment, Problems 34–39
4c	**Developing Goal** Use an algorithm to add and subtract mixed numbers having fractions with unlike denominators. (Lesson 4.5)	Written Assessment, Problems 17, 18, 19b, and 30–33
4d	**Developing Goal** Use an algorithm to subtract mixed numbers having fractions with like denominators. (Lesson 4.4)	Written Assessment, Problems 27, 28, and 29
4e	**Developing Goal** Find a percent of a number. (Lesson 4.11)	Slate Assessment, Problem 4
4f	**Secure Goal** Use an algorithm to add mixed numbers having fractions with like denominators. (Lesson 4.4)	Written Assessment, Problem 26
4g	**Secure Goal** Use an algorithm to add and subtract fractions with like and unlike denominators. (Lesson 4.3)	Oral Assessment, Problems 1 and 2 Written Assessment, Problems 19a and 21–25
4h	**Secure Goal** Compare and order fractions. (Lesson 4.2)	Oral Assessment, Problem 1 Slate Assessment, Problem 3 Written Assessment, Problems 20 and 21
4i	**Secure Goal** Convert between fractions, mixed numbers, decimals, and percents. (Lessons 4.1, 4.3–4.5, and 4.7–4.9)	Slate Assessment, Problems 2, 5, and 6 Written Assessment, Problems 5–16 and 40
4j	**Secure Goal** Write fractions and mixed numbers in simplest form. (Lessons 4.1 and 4.4)	Slate Assessment, Problem 1 Written Assessment, Problems 1–4 and 22–39

Alternative Assessment

In Lesson 4.12, you will find alternative assessment options on pages 276 and 277.

✦ Write and Solve Fraction Number Stories

Students write and solve number stories involving addition, subtraction, and multiplication of fractions and mixed numbers. As you circulate to check students' work, keep these questions in mind:

Portfolio Ideas

- Is the story complete? Are all of the numbers in the problem used? Is a question posed?
- Does the number story reflect an understanding of the fraction or mixed-number computation involved?
- Can the student solve the problem correctly?

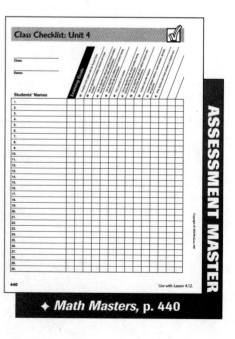

✦ *Math Masters*, p. 440

✦ Describe a Fraction or Mixed-Number Computation Strategy

Students are given a fraction or mixed-number addition, subtraction, or multiplication problem. Students first solve the problem, then describe the strategy they used. As you circulate to check students' work, keep these questions in mind:

- Did the student correctly solve the problem?
- Did the description match the work that the student did?
- Does the student's work reflect an understanding of the computation involved?

✦ Play *Spoon Scramble*

Students make a set of cards, using Activity Sheets 1 or 2, or they use index cards. They play the game with a partner. As students play the game, keep these questions in mind:

- Can the student add fractions?
- Can the student multiply fractions?
- Is the student able to convert between fractions and mixed or whole numbers?
- Can the student name fractions in simplest form?

Date _____ Time _____

Spoon Scramble Cards 1

$\frac{1}{7}$ of 42	$\frac{24}{4} * \frac{5}{5}$	$\frac{54}{9}$	$2\frac{16}{4}$
$\frac{1}{5}$ of 35	$\frac{21}{3} * \frac{4}{4}$	$\frac{56}{8}$	$4\frac{36}{12}$
$\frac{1}{8}$ of 64	$\frac{48}{6} * \frac{3}{3}$	$\frac{32}{4}$	$3\frac{25}{5}$
$\frac{1}{4}$ of 36	$\frac{63}{7} * \frac{6}{6}$	$\frac{72}{8}$	$5\frac{32}{8}$

Use with Lesson 4.12.   **Activity Sheet 1**

STUDENT PAGE

✦ *Math Journal 1*, Activity Sheet 1

Unit 5
Assessment Overview

At this point in the *Everyday Mathematics* program, you may wish to consider whether you are beginning to establish a balance of Ongoing, Product, and Periodic Assessment strategies. Also, think about whether your strategies include both anecdotal records based on observations of students' progress and the use of written assessments.

Ongoing Assessment Opportunities

Ongoing assessment provides opportunities to observe students during regular interactions as they work independently and in groups. You can conduct ongoing assessment during teacher-guided instruction, Math Boxes sessions, mathematical mini-interviews, games, Mental Math and Reflexes sessions, strategy sharing, and slate work. The chart below provides a summary of ongoing assessment opportunities in Unit 5 as they relate to specific Unit 5 learning goals.

5a **Developing Goal** Apply properties of supplementary angles and vertical angles. (Lessons 5.2, 5.9, and 5.10)	Lesson 5.9, p. 331
5b **Developing Goal** Apply properties of angles formed by two parallel lines and a transversal. (Lessons 5.9 and 5.10)	Lesson 5.9, p. 331
5d **Developing Goal** Calculate the degree measure of each sector in a circle graph and use a protractor to construct the graph. (Lesson 5.3)	Lesson 5.3, pp. 300 and 302
5f **Developing/Secure Goal** Apply properties of sums of angle measures of triangles and quadrangles. (Lessons 5.2 and 5.9)	Lesson 5.2, p. 297

Product Assessment Opportunities

Math Journals, Math Boxes, Activity Sheets, *Math Masters,* math logs, and the results of Projects all provide product assessment opportunities. Here is an example of how you might use a rubric to assess students' ability to identify parallel lines.

Lesson 5.11, p. 344

ALTERNATIVE ASSESSMENT Identify Parallel Lines

Most of your students should be able to decide that the
two lines are not parallel, but ability levels will vary.
Some students may not realize that they should draw a
transversal and measure the angles formed to check
whether the lines are parallel. Use your own rubric, or the sample
rubric below, to evaluate students' work.

(Portfolio Ideas)

Sample Rubric
Beginning (B)   The student identifies the two lines as not parallel but has difficulty proving or justifying his or her answer. The student may try to extend the lines or try to measure the distance between the two lines. The written explanation is incomplete.
Developing (D)   The student identifies the two lines as not parallel. The student explains his or her thinking clearly, stating that he or she measured the distance between the lines. The student may also have to extend the lines to justify the solution.
Secure (S)   The student identifies the two lines as not parallel. The student clearly communicates his or her understanding by drawing a transversal and measuring the angles. The student applies knowledge from Lesson 5.9 of supplementary, adjacent, and vertical angles in his or her explanation, clearly demonstrating an understanding of these concepts.

Periodic Assessment Opportunities

Here is a summary of the periodic assessment opportunities that
are provided in Unit 5. Refer to Lesson 5.11 for details.

Oral and Slate Assessment

In Lesson 5.11, you will find oral and slate assessment problems on
pages 342 and 343.

Written Assessment

In Lesson 5.11, you will find written assessment problems on
pages 343 and 344 (*Math Masters,* pages 400–402).

See the chart below to find oral, slate, and written assessment
problems that address specific learning goals.

5a **Developing Goal** Apply properties of supplementary angles and vertical angles. (Lessons 5.2, 5.9, and 5.10)	Written Assessment, Problems 7–12
5b **Developing Goal** Apply properties of angles formed by two parallel lines and a transversal. (Lessons 5.9 and 5.10)	Written Assessment, Problem 9
5c **Developing Goal** Apply properties of angles of parallelograms. (Lesson 5.10)	Written Assessment, Problems 10 and 11
5d **Developing Goal** Calculate the degree measure of each sector in a circle graph and use a protractor to make the graph. (Lesson 5.3)	Slate Assessment, Problem 2 Written Assessment, Problem 13

5e	**Developing Goal** Use a compass and straightedge to construct geometric figures. (Lessons 5.7 and 5.8)	Written Assessment, Problem 14
5f	**Developing/Secure Goal** Apply properties of sums of angle measures of triangles and quadrangles. (Lessons 5.2 and 5.9)	Oral Assessment, Problem 1 Written Assessment, Problems 11 and 12
5g	**Secure Goal** Translate figures on a coordinate grid. (Lessons 5.4–5.6)	Written Assessment, Problem 6
5h	**Secure Goal** Plot ordered number pairs in four quadrants; use ordered number pairs to name points in four quadrants. (Lesson 5.4)	Written Assessment, Problem 6
5i	**Secure Goal** Draw or form a figure congruent to a given figure. (Lessons 5.5 and 5.6)	Oral Assessment, Problem 2 Written Assessment, Problem 6
5j	**Secure Goal** Classify angles. (Lessons 5.1 and 5.2)	Slate Assessment, Problem 1 Written Assessment, Problems 7 and 8
5k	**Secure Goal** Measure and draw angles using a protractor. (Lesson 5.1)	Oral Assessment, Problem 1 Written Assessment, Problems 1–5

Alternative Assessment

In Lesson 5.11, you will find alternative assessment options on pages 344 and 345.

✦ Identify Parallel Lines

Use *Math Masters,* page 91, to assess students' understanding of properties of parallel lines. As students work, keep the following questions in mind:

Portfolio Ideas

• Does the student use a valid method, such as drawing a transversal and measuring angles, to decide whether the lines are parallel?
• Or does the student try (unsuccessfully) to extend the lines to see whether they meet?
• Or does the student try (unsuccessfully) to measure various distances between the lines?

✦ Sort Shapes

Students sort shapes according to properties they choose. As students work, keep these questions in mind:

Portfolio Ideas

• Is the student correctly sorting the shapes?
• Can the student sort the shapes in more than one way?

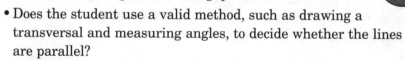

✦ *Math Masters, p. 442*

Unit 6
Assessment Overview

The focus of this unit is preparing students for algebra and solving equations. Goal 6b is an important part of this preparation. The goal chart below shows ongoing assessment opportunities for observing students as they develop this skill. The chart shows that ongoing assessment opportunities related to Goal 6b can be found in Lessons 6.8, 6.9, 6.10, and 6.11 on pages 497, 500, 510, and 514 respectively of your *Teacher's Lesson Guide*. The chart on page 57 indicates where you can find slate and written problems to help you assess students' progress toward this same goal.

Ongoing Assessment Opportunities

Ongoing assessment provides opportunities to observe students during regular interactions as they work independently and in groups. You can conduct ongoing assessment during teacher-guided instruction, Math Boxes sessions, mathematical mini-interviews, games, Mental Math and Reflexes sessions, strategy sharing, and slate work. The chart below provides a summary of ongoing assessment opportunities in Unit 6 as they relate to specific Unit 6 learning goals.

6b **Developing Goal** Solve equations. (Lessons 6.8–6.11)	Lesson 6.8, p. 497 Lesson 6.9, p. 500 Lesson 6.10, p. 510 Lesson 6.11, p. 514
6c **Developing Goal** Use an algorithm to add, subtract, multiply, and divide fractions and mixed numbers. (Lessons 6.1 and 6.2)	Lesson 6.2, p. 460
6e **Developing/Secure Goal** Add, subtract, multiply, and divide integers. (Lessons 6.3 and 6.4)	Lesson 6.3, p. 467 Lesson 6.4, p. 473
6f **Developing/Secure Goal** Understand and apply order of operations to evaluate expressions and solve number sentences. (Lessons 6.6 and 6.8)	Lesson 6.6, p. 484
6g **Developing/Secure Goal** Determine whether number sentences are true or false. (Lesson 6.7)	Lesson 6.7, p. 489

Product Assessment Opportunities

Math Journals, Math Boxes, Activity Sheets, *Math Masters,* math logs, and the results of Projects all provide product assessment opportunities. Here is an example of how you might use a rubric to assess students' ability to solve pan-balance problems.

Lesson 6.9, p. 506

EXTRA PRACTICE **Solving Pan-Balance Problems**

Most of your students should be able to solve the types of problems suggested on page 506 of your *Teacher's Lesson Guide.* Prepare a page of problems, using those as models. Use your own rubric, or the sample rubric below, to evaluate students' work.

Portfolio Ideas

Sample Rubric

Beginning (B)
The student requires teacher assistance to solve the pan-balance problems. The use of the pan balance or manipulatives may be necessary to work through each problem. The student has difficulty thinking algebraically and is unable to think abstractly.

Developing (D)
The student solves the pan-balance problems with partial or satisfactory understanding and with only minor errors. The student exhibits that he or she is able to apply algebraic understanding to similar problems.

Secure (S)
The student solves the pan-balance problems independently. The student's work reflects good algebraic thinking. The student is capable of making connections from the problems given in order to solve more complicated problems.

Periodic Assessment Opportunities

Here is a summary of the periodic assessment opportunities that are provided in Unit 6. Refer to Lesson 6.13 for details.

Oral and Slate Assessment

In Lesson 6.13, you will find oral and slate assessment problems on pages 524 and 525.

Written Assessment

In Lesson 6.13, you will find written assessment problems on pages 525 and 526 (*Math Masters,* pages 403–405).

See the following chart to find oral, slate, and written assessment problems that address specific learning goals.

6a	**Beginning Goal** Solve and graph solutions for inequalities. (Lesson 6.12)	Written Assessment, Problems 53–55
6b	**Developing Goal** Solve equations. (Lessons 6.8–6.11)	Slate Assessment, Problem 4 Written Assessment, Problems 39–52
6c	**Developing Goal** Use an algorithm to add, subtract, multiply, and divide fractions and mixed numbers. (Lessons 6.1 and 6.2)	Oral Assessment, Problem 1 Slate Assessment, Problem 2 Written Assessment, Problems 1, 8, 9, and 20–29
6d	**Developing/Secure Goal** Find opposites and reciprocals of numbers. (Lessons 6.1 and 6.2)	Slate Assessment, Problem 1 Written Assessment, Problems 18, 19, and 23
6e	**Developing/Secure Goal** Add, subtract, multiply, and divide integers. (Lessons 6.3 and 6.4)	Written Assessment, Problems 4–7, 10–20, 25, and 33
6f	**Developing/Secure Goal** Understand and apply order of operations to evaluate expressions and solve number sentences. (Lessons 6.6 and 6.8)	Written Assessment, Problems 1 and 31–38
6g	**Developing/Secure Goal** Determine whether number sentences are true or false. (Lesson 6.7)	Written Assessment, Problem 1
6h	**Secure Goal** Compare and order integers. (Lesson 6.3)	Written Assessment, Problems 2–7
6i	**Secure Goal** Understand and apply the identity property for multiplication. (Lessons 6.4 and 6.5)	Written Assessment, Problem 1
6j	**Secure Goal** Understand and apply the commutative property for addition and multiplication. (Lessons 6.1 and 6.3)	Written Assessment, Problem 1
6k	**Secure Goal** Understand and apply the associative property for addition and multiplication. (Lessons 6.3–6.5)	Written Assessment, Problems 1 and 30

Alternative Assessment

In Lesson 6.13, you will find alternative assessment options on page 526.

✦ Explore Scientific Calculators

This activity is intended to assess students' knowledge of the order of operations. Students enter a series of operations into a scientific and a nonscientific calculator, then determine how the calculator performed the operations. As students work, keep these questions in mind:

• Does the student recognize that the scientific calculator is performing the operations in the correct order of operations? That the nonscientific calculator is not performing the operations in the correct order of operations?

• Can the student write the correct number sentence for the order of operations being performed by each calculation?

Class Checklist: Unit 6

Class _____

Dates _____

Students' Names

Learning Goals

1.
2.
3.
4.
5.
6.
7.
8.
9.
10.
11.
12.
13.
14.
15.
16.
17.
18.
19.
20.
21.
22.
23.
24.
25.
26.
27.
28.
29.
30.

444   Use with Lesson 6.13.

ASSESSMENT MASTER

✦ Math Masters, p. 444

✦ Play *Name That Number*

This game helps you assess a student's ability to solve equations and his or her understanding of the order of operations. As students play the game, keep these questions in mind:

• Can the student write a correct number sentence for each target number?

• Is the student able to use a large number of numbers and multiple operations to make each target number?

✦ Solve Pan-Balance Problems

This activity helps you assess a student's facility with using the pan-balance model to solve equations. Use a Class Checklist or calendar grids to record students' progress. As students work, keep these questions in mind:

• Does the student consistently perform the same operation to each side of the balance?

• Does the student perform the operations necessary to answer the question that is posed?

• Can the student work problems that involve multiple operations?

• Is the student able to deal with Problems 8–10, which involve variables?

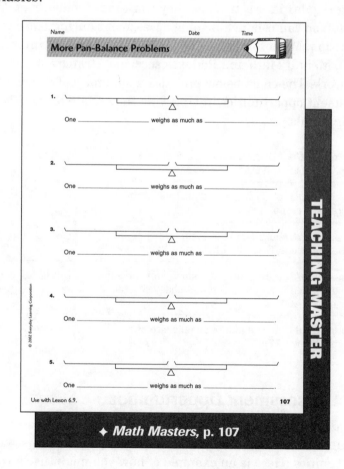

✦ *Math Masters*, p. 107

Unit 7
Assessment Overview

In this unit, students continue their study of probability. Depending on the specific skill, a student's ability levels might range from Beginning to Secure. A good mix of ongoing assessment opportunities is suggested in the chart below for several learning goals that deal with probability. Written and slate assessments for these same goals are listed in the chart on pages 59 and 60.

Ongoing Assessment Opportunities

Ongoing assessment provides opportunities to observe students during regular interactions as they work independently and in groups. You can conduct ongoing assessment during teacher-guided instruction, Math Boxes sessions, mathematical mini-interviews, games, Mental Math and Reflexes sessions, strategy sharing, and slate work. The chart below provides a summary of ongoing assessment opportunities in Unit 7 as they relate to specific Unit 7 learning goals.

7a **Beginning Goal** Understand and use tree diagrams to solve problems. (Lesson 7.4, 7.5, and 7.7)	Lesson 7.4, p. 559 Lesson 7.5, p. 565
7b **Developing Goal** Construct and interpret Venn diagrams. (Lesson 7.6)	Lesson 7.6, p. 569
7c **Developing/Secure Goal** Calculate probability in simple situations. (Lessons 7.1, 7.3, and 7.4)	Lesson 7.1, p. 541
7e **Developing/Secure Goal** Understand and apply the concept of random numbers to probability situations. (Lessons 7.2 and 7.3)	Lesson 7.3, p. 554
7g **Secure Goal** Understand how sample size affects results. (Lesson 7.2)	Lesson 7.2, p. 549

Product Assessment Opportunities

Math Journals, Math Boxes, Activity Sheets, *Math Masters,* math logs, and the results of Projects all provide product assessment opportunities. Here is an example of how you might use a rubric to assess a student's ability to work probability problems.

ALTERNATIVE ASSESSMENT Make a Fair Game

Most of your students should be able to determine how to make the *Sum Game* fair. Use *Math Masters,* page 125 to assess students' understanding of applying probability concepts. Use your own rubric, or the sample rubric below, to evaluate students' work.

Portfolio Ideas

Sample Rubric

Beginning (B)
The small group or partnership of students experiences difficulty in getting started with the activity. Teacher assistance is required and prompts are needed throughout. The group applies inappropriate strategies and does not make the necessary connections. For example, they may not play several rounds of the game in order to make an actual estimate for the different scores OR they do not make a tree diagram. As a result, they are unable to determine how to make the *Sum Game* fair and have difficulty communicating the strategies utilized.

Developing (D)
The small group or partnership of students attempts to solve the problem, but some teacher assistance may be required. The group demonstrates satisfactory understanding of applying probability concepts. It is able to make connections by applying its knowledge of making tree diagrams or by playing the game repeatedly, and estimating the probabilities of the different scores to the *Sum Game*. The group communicates the strategies used to make the game fair with some needed refining from the teacher.

Secure (S)
The small group or partnership of students attempts the problem without any teacher assistance required. The group applies its knowledge of probability concepts and makes connections with appropriate strategies. The group uses the tree diagram to illustrate clearly how to make the *Sum Game* fair. As a result, the group communicates clearly and effectively how and why it solved the problem.

Periodic Assessment Opportunities

Here is a summary of the periodic assessment opportunities that are provided in Unit 7. Refer to Lesson 7.9 for details.

Oral and Slate Assessment

In Lesson 7.9, you will find oral and slate assessment problems on pages 586 and 587.

Written Assessment

In Lesson 7.9, you will find written assessment problems on pages 587 and 588 (*Math Masters,* pages 406–409).

See the chart below and on the next page to find slate and written assessment problems that address specific learning goals.

7a	**Beginning Goal** Understand and use tree diagrams to solve problems. (Lessons 7.4, 7.5, and 7.7)	Written Assessment, Problems 12 and 14–17
7b	**Developing Goal** Construct and interpret Venn diagrams. (Lesson 7.6)	Written Assessment, Problem 22
7c	**Developing/Secure Goal** Calculate probability in simple situations. (Lessons 7.1, 7.3, and 7.4)	Written Assessment, Problems 8–11, 13, 14, and 18–20

7d **Developing/Secure Goal** Understand what constitutes a fair game. (Lesson 7.7)	Written Assessment, Problems 16 and 17
7e **Developing/Secure Goal** Understand and apply the concept of random numbers to probability situations. (Lessons 7.2 and 7.3)	Written Assessment, Problems 8–11
7f **Secure Goal** Solve "fraction-of-a-fraction" problems. (Lesson 7.3)	Slate Assessment, Problem 2 Written Assessment, Problems 1–7
7g **Secure Goal** Understand how sample size affects results. (Lesson 7.2)	Written Assessment, Problem 21

Alternative Assessment

In Lesson 7.9, you will find alternative assessment options on pages 588 and 589.

✦ Predict the Number and Colors of Blocks in a Bag

Students make repeated draws from a bag to predict the colors of the blocks in the bag. As students work, keep these questions in mind:

- Does the student see that the fewer the blocks in the bag, the easier his or her prediction is?
- Does the student see that the more draws that are made, the greater the chance that he or she can accurately predict the contents of the bag?

✦ Make a Fair Game

Students work in a group to make an unfair game fair. As you circulate to check students' work, keep these questions in mind:

- Does the group understand how to find the probability of each score?
- Does the group's solution show an understanding of what makes a game fair?

✦ Make Venn Diagrams from Internet Searches

Students work in pairs to create Venn diagrams that describe an Internet search. Have students draw their diagrams on a sheet of paper that you can collect and assess. As you check their papers, keep these questions in mind:

- Can the pair describe an Internet search that gets them the information that is required?
- Can they draw a diagram to represent the Internet search they've planned?

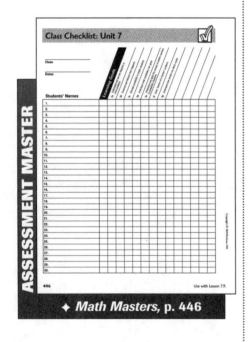

ASSESSMENT MASTER

Class Checklist: Unit 7

Class

Dates

Students' Names

446   Use with Lesson 7.9.

✦ Math Masters, p. 446

Unit 8
Assessment Overview

In this unit, students develop their skills with ratios, proportions, and percent. By this time, perhaps you have tried several different types of assessment strategies. Remember, as you use a balance of assessment approaches, the overall effectiveness of your assessment plan should improve. If there is still a major type of assessment, such as Ongoing, Product, or Periodic, that you haven't used, this unit might be a good time to try it.

Ongoing Assessment Opportunities

Ongoing assessment provides opportunities to observe students during regular interactions as they work independently and in groups. You can conduct ongoing assessment during teacher-guided instruction, Math Boxes sessions, mathematical mini-interviews, games, Mental Math and Reflexes sessions, strategy sharing, and slate work. The chart below provides a summary of ongoing assessment opportunities in Unit 8 as they relate to specific Unit 8 learning goals.

8b **Developing Goal** Solve percent problems. (Lessons 8.5, 8.7, and 8.8)	Lesson 8.7, p. 644
8c **Developing Goal** Solve problems involving a size-change factor. (Lessons 8.9 and 8.10)	Lesson 8.9, p. 656
8d **Developing/Secure Goal** Use cross-multiplication to solve open proportions. (Lessons 8.3, 8.6, and 8.7)	Lesson 8.3, p. 619 Lesson 8.7, p. 644
8e **Developing/Secure Goal** Solve rate number stories. (Lessons 8.1–8.5)	Lesson 8.1, pp. 605 and 606 Lesson 8.4, p. 623
8f **Developing/Secure Goal** Solve ratio number stories. (Lessons 8.6, 8.9, 8.11, and 8.12)	Lesson 8.6, p. 639
8g **Developing/Secure Goal** Estimate equivalent percents for fractions. (Lesson 8.8)	Lesson 8.8, p. 650
8h **Developing/Secure Goal** Solve division problems involving decimals. (Lessons 8.9 and 8.11)	Lesson 8.10, p. 664 Lesson 8.11, p. 672
8i **Secure Goal** Use rate tables to solve problems. (Lessons 8.1 and 8.2)	Lesson 8.1, pp. 605 and 606 Lesson 8.4, p. 623

Product Assessment Opportunities

Journals, Math Boxes, Activity Sheets, *Math Masters,* math logs, and the results of Projects all provide product assessment opportunities. Here is an example of how you might use a rubric to assess students' ability to solve rate problems.

Lesson 8.3, p. 620

EXTRA PRACTICE **Calculating Amounts of Ingredients for Making Peanut Butter Fudge**

Most of your students should be able to calculate amounts of ingredients needed for 1 pound and 80 pounds, but abilities will vary. Some students may be able to find correct answers for the whole numbers but experience difficulty when presented with fractions or mixed numbers. Use your own rubric, or the sample rubric below, to evaluate students' work.

> **Portfolio Ideas**

Sample Rubric

Beginning (B)
The student has difficulty in getting started, and teacher assistance is required. The student may select inappropriate strategies, displaying a lack of understanding of rates and proportions. He or she does not make appropriate connections with the clues that are given in order to solve the problems. As a result, most of the answers given are incorrect.

Developing (D)
The student attempts to solve the problems independently. Some assistance may be required, especially on problems in which fractions or mixed numbers are involved. The student demonstrates satisfactory understanding of rates and proportions. He or she makes connections with the clues that are given and applies appropriate strategies to solve the problems. As a result, the student is able to solve most of the problems.

Secure (S)
The student attempts to solve the problems without teacher assistance. The student demonstrates a strong understanding of rates and proportions and is able to make the necessary connections using the clues given, even when using fractions and mixed numbers. He or she applies appropriate strategies in order to solve the problems. As a result, the problems are solved correctly.

Periodic Assessment Opportunities

Here is a summary of the periodic assessment opportunities that are provided in Unit 8. Refer to Lesson 8.13 for details.

Oral and Slate Assessment

In Lesson 8.13, you will find oral and slate assessment problems on pages 681 and 682.

Written Assessment

In Lesson 8.13, you will find written assessment problems on page 683 (*Math Masters,* pages 410–413).

See the chart on the next page to find slate and written assessment problems that address specific learning goals.

8a	**Developing Goal** Write open proportions to model problems. (Lessons 8.1, 8.2, and 8.6)	Written Assessment, Problems 12–17
8b	**Developing Goal** Solve percent problems. (Lessons 8.5, 8.7, and 8.8)	Slate Assessment, Problem 3 Written Assessment, Problems 16–19 and 23
8c	**Developing Goal** Solve problems involving a size-change factor. (Lessons 8.9 and 8.10)	Written Assessment, Problems 26–29
8d	**Developing/Secure Goal** Use cross-multiplication to solve open proportions. (Lessons 8.3, 8.6, and 8.7)	Written Assessment, Problems 8–13
8e	**Developing/Secure Goal** Solve rate number stories. (Lessons 8.1–8.5)	Written Assessment, Problems 1–4 and 12–15
8f	**Developing/Secure Goal** Solve ratio number stories. (Lessons 8.6, 8.9, 8.11, and 8.12)	Written Assessment, Problems 16, 17, and 20–29
8g	**Developing/Secure Goal** Estimate equivalent percents for fractions. (Lesson 8.8)	Slate Assessment, Problem 4 Written Assessment, Problems 18 and 19
8h	**Developing/Secure Goal** Solve division problems involving decimals. (Lessons 8.9 and 8.11)	Written Assessment, Problems 30 and 31
8i	**Secure Goal** Use rate tables to solve problems. (Lessons 8.1 and 8.2)	Written Assessment, Problems 1, 2, 12, and 13

Alternative Assessment

In Lesson 8.13, you will find alternative assessment options on pages 683 and 684.

✦ Write Ratio Number Stories

This activity is intended to assess a student's skill at writing ratio number stories. Consider the following questions:

- Is the story complete? (Is information given and a question posed?)
- Does the number story ask a question that can be answered using the information given?
- Does the number story reflect an understanding of ratios?

✦ Enlarge a Picture

Students draw a grid on a picture and then copy the picture, using a larger grid. Use a Class Checklist or calendar grids to record students' progress. As students work, keep these questions in mind:

- Is the student able to draw the enlarged picture?
- Does the student understand what size-change factor was used to make the enlarged drawing?

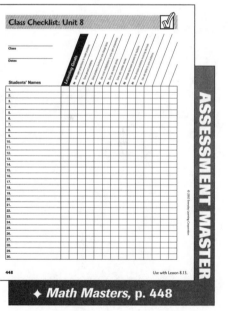

✦ *Math Masters*, p. 448

Unit 9
Assessment Overview

As you near the end of the Sixth Grade *Everyday Mathematics* program, reflect on your success in developing a balanced assessment plan. Think about which assessment strategies worked best. Are there strategies that you did not have time to try this year but which you would like to try next year? To help you remember them next fall, record your thoughts on the note pages in this book.

Ongoing Assessment Opportunities

Ongoing assessment provides opportunities to observe students during regular interactions as they work independently and in groups. You can conduct ongoing assessment during teacher-guided instruction, Math Boxes sessions, mathematical mini-interviews, games, Mental Math and Reflexes sessions, strategy sharing, and slate work. The chart below provides a summary of ongoing assessment opportunities in Unit 9 as they relate to specific Unit 9 learning goals.

9a **Developing Goal** Simplify expressions and equations with parentheses. (Lessons 9.4 and 9.5)	Lesson 9.5, p. 723
9b **Developing/Secure Goal** Apply the distributive property. (Lessons 9.1, 9.2, 9.4, and 9.5)	Lesson 9.4, p. 717
9c **Developing/Secure Goal** Combine like terms to simplify expressions and equations. (Lessons 9.3–9.5)	Lesson 9.3, p. 713
9d **Developing/Secure Goal** Solve equations. (Lessons 9.5, 9.6, and 9.10)	Lesson 9.10, p. 752
9f **Developing/Secure Goal** Write and solve equations that represent problem situations. (Lessons 9.1, 9.5, 9.6, and 9.11)	Lesson 9.6, p. 728
9g **Developing/Secure Goal** Use formulas to solve problems. (Lessons 9.8, 9.9, and 9.11)	Lesson 9.8, p. 739 Lesson 9.11, p. 757
9h **Secure Goal** Evaluate expressions and formulas. (Lessons 9.3, 9.4, 9.8, 9.9, 9.11, and 9.12)	Lesson 9.8, p. 739 Lesson 9.11, p. 757

Product Assessment Opportunities

Journals, Math Boxes, Activity Sheets, *Math Masters,* math logs, and the results of Projects all provide product assessment opportunities. Here is an example of how you might use a rubric to assess students' ability to write number stories involving the distributive property.

Lesson 9.14, p. 776

ALTERNATIVE ASSESSMENT Write Number Stories Involving the Distributive Property

Most of your students should be able to write a number story for each of the expressions. Student abilities will vary. Use your own rubric, or the sample rubric below, to evaluate students' work.

 Portfolio Ideas

Sample Rubric

Beginning (B)
The student experiences difficulty attempting to write a number story for any of the expressions on journal page 343. Teacher assistance is required. As a result, the student writes inappropriate number stories which display a lack of understanding of the distributive property.

Developing (D)
The student attempts to write number stories for the expressions given on journal page 343. Satisfactory understanding of the distributive property is displayed when the student applies his or her knowledge to write number stories that connect to the expressions. Some teacher assistance is required.

Secure (S)
The student independently writes number stories, using the expressions on journal page 343. The number stories reflect a strong understanding of the distributive property and the ability to make connections between the expressions and number stories. He or she also applies the distributive property in new situations by selecting expressions that use variables.

Periodic Assessment Opportunities

Here is a summary of the periodic assessment opportunities that are provided in Unit 9. Refer to Lesson 9.14 for details.

Oral and Slate Assessment

In Lesson 9.14, you will find oral and slate assessment problems on pages 774 and 775.

Written Assessment

In Lesson 9.14, you will find written assessment problems on page 776 (*Math Masters,* pages 414–417).

See the chart on the next page to find slate and written assessment problems that address specific learning goals.

9a **Developing Goal** Simplify expressions and equations with parentheses. (Lessons 9.4 and 9.5)	Written Assessment, Problems 8, 9, 11, and 12
9b **Developing/Secure Goal** Apply the distributive property. (Lessons 9.1, 9.2, 9.4, and 9.5)	Slate Assessment, Problem 4 Written Assessment, Problems 1, 2, 8, 9, 11, and 12
9c **Developing/Secure Goal** Combine like terms to simplify expressions and equations. (Lessons 9.3–9.5)	Slate Assessment, Problem 4 Written Assessment, Problems 2, 5–10, and 13
9d **Developing/Secure Goal** Solve equations. (Lessons 9.5, 9.6, and 9.10)	Written Assessment, Problems 10–13 and 28
9e **Developing/Secure Goal** Write and identify equivalent expressions and equivalent equations. (Lessons 9.3–9.5)	Slate Assessment, Problem 4 Written Assessment, Problems 5–13 and 16
9f **Developing/Secure Goal** Write and solve equations that represent problem situations. (Lessons 9.1, 9.5, 9.6, and 9.11)	Written Assessment, Problems 2 and 23–27
9g **Developing/Secure Goal** Use formulas to solve problems. (Lessons 9.8, 9.9, and 9.11)	Written Assessment, Problems 2–4, 14, 15, and 17–27
9h **Secure Goal** Evaluate expressions and formulas. (Lessons 9.3, 9.4, 9.8, 9.9, 9.11, and 9.12)	Slate Assessment, Problem 2 Written Assessment, Problems 3, 4, 14, 15, and 17–27

Alternative Assessment

In Lesson 9.14, you will find alternative assessment options on pages 776 and 777.

✦ Write Number Stories Involving the Distributive Property

Students are given expressions and then write number stories to fit the expressions. As you circulate to check students' work, use a Class Checklist or calendar grids to record their progress. Keep the following questions in mind:

- Is the number story complete? (Is information given and a question posed?)
- Does the number story ask a question that can be answered using the information given?
- Does the number story fit the expression that was given?

Class Checklist: Unit 9

Class

Dates

Students' Names

450   Use with Lesson 9.14.

✦ **Math Masters, p. 450**

✦ Interpret an Algebra Cartoon

Students interpret an algebra cartoon. Use this activity to assess students' understanding of variables. As you evaluate student work, keep the following questions in mind:

- Does the student understand that a variable may have a single correct value?
- Does the student understand that the same variable may have one correct value in one equation and another correct value in a different equation?
- Does the student understand that a variable may not always have one correct value? For example, $x < 2$ has many solutions.

✦ Explore the Area of Parallelograms and Triangles

Students cut out parallelograms and triangles that are drawn on centimeter grids. They cut the shapes apart and rearrange them as rectangles and parallelograms respectively. Then they find areas. As you discuss the problem with the class, keep the following questions in mind:

- Was the student able to identify the bases and heights of the parallelograms and triangles? The lengths and widths of the rectangles?
- Could the student find the areas of all the shapes?
- Could the student explain why the area formulas work?

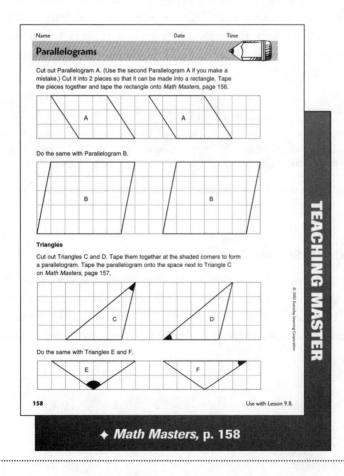

✦ *Math Masters, p. 158*

Unit 10
Assessment Overview

Looking back over the Sixth Grade *Everyday Mathematics* program, have you been able to establish a balance of Ongoing, Product, and Periodic Assessment strategies? Have your strategies included keeping anecdotal records based on observations of student's progress, as well as the use of written assessments? This might be a good time to evaluate your assessment strategies and think of what approaches you might consider for next year.

Ongoing Assessment Opportunities

Ongoing assessment provides opportunities to observe students during regular interactions as they work independently and in groups. You can conduct ongoing assessment during teacher-guided instruction, Math Boxes sessions, mathematical mini-interviews, games, Mental Math and Reflexes sessions, strategy sharing, and slate work. The chart below provides a summary of ongoing assessment opportunities in Unit 10 as they relate to specific Unit 10 learning goals.

10a **Beginning Goal** Identify and use notation for semiregular tessellations. (Lesson 10.1)	Lesson 10.1, p. 792
10d **Beginning Goal** Explore rotation and point symmetry. (Lesson 10.3)	Lesson 10.3, p. 803
10f **Beginning Goal** Perform topological transformations. (Lessons 10.5 and 10.6)	Lesson 10.5, p. 814

Product Assessment Opportunities

Math Journals, Math Boxes, Activity Sheets, *Math Masters,* math logs, and the results of Projects all provide product assessment opportunities. On the next page is an example of how you might use a rubric to assess students' ability to draw regular tessellations.

Lesson 10.1, p. 794

RETEACHING Exploring Regular Tessellations

Most of your students should be able to tessellate the
triangle, square, and hexagon, but ability levels will
vary. Some students may think that they have
tessellated the pentagon when they have not. Use your
own rubric, or the sample rubric below, to evaluate students' work.

Portfolio Ideas

Sample Rubric

Beginning (B)
The student experiences difficulty starting the activity due to a lack of an understanding of
tessellations. Teacher assistance is required. The student is encouraged to use the polygon
cutouts that are provided. As a result, some of the answers are incorrect, as reflected in the
illustrations drawn in *Math Masters,* page 169. The student struggles especially with the
pentagon and hexagon.

Developing (D)
The student attempts to solve the problems independently, using the polygon cutouts.
Although the student may display satisfactory understanding of tessellations, a few answers
or illustrations might be incorrect but are easily corrected with some teacher guidance.

Secure (S)
The student displays a solid understanding of tessellations by solving the problems in *Math
Masters,* page 169 independently, using the polygon cut-outs. The student may also take the
activity a step further by making connections and labeling each regular tessellation using the
3.3.3.3.3.3., 4.4.4.4., or 6.6.6. labeling method.

Periodic Assessment Opportunities

Here is a summary of the periodic assessment opportunities that
are provided in Unit 10. Refer to Lesson 10.7 for details.

Oral and Slate Assessment

In Lesson 10.7, you will find oral and slate assessment problems on
pages 824 and 825.

Written Assessment

In Lesson 10.7, you will find written assessment problems on
page 825 (*Math Masters,* pages 418 and 419).

See the chart on the next page to find oral, slate, and written
assessment problems that address specific learning goals.

10a **Beginning Goal** Identify and use notation for semiregular tessellations. (Lesson 10.1)	Written Assessment, Problems 4 and 5
10b **Beginning Goal** Identify regular tessellations. (Lesson 10.1)	Written Assessment, Problems 2 and 3
10c **Beginning Goal** Create nonpolygonal, translation tessellations. (Lesson 10.2)	Written Assessment, Problem 9
10d **Beginning Goal** Explore rotation and point symmetry. (Lesson 10.3)	Written Assessment, Problem 10
10e **Beginning Goal** Discover properties of solids. (Lesson 10.4)	Oral Assessment, Problem 2 Slate Assessment, Problem 1 Written Assessment, Problems 6–8
10f **Beginning Goal** Perform topological transformations. (Lessons 10.5 and 10.6)	Written Assessment, Problem 1

ASSESSMENT MASTER

Class Checklist: Unit 10

Class

Dates

Students' Names

452   Use with Lesson 10.7.

◆ *Math Masters, p. 452*

Alternative Assessment

In Lesson 10.7, you will find alternative assessment options on pages 825 and 826.

✦ Make Tessellation Designs

Students make and color designs that involve symmetry, then label the symmetry. As you circulate to check students' work, keep these questions in mind:

• Did the student make a symmetrical design?

• Was the student able to correctly identify the type of symmetry for his or her design?

• Was the student able to draw correctly a design with more than one type of symmetry?

✦ Write Reports

Students write 4 paragraphs on any one of a list of topics. As you circulate to check students' work, keep these questions in mind:

• Does the student have a clear grasp of the facts?

• Does the report include the most important aspects of the topic?

• Is the student's writing clear and consistent?

Assessment Masters

How to Use the Masters

NOTE: This page provides a brief summary of how the general Assessment Masters may be used. The uses of these masters are described in more detail near the front of this book on pages 3–29.

The *Assessment Handbook* contains reduced versions of all of the Assessment Masters found in your *Math Masters* book. You can use these reduced pages to assist you in developing your assessment plan. The following general masters may be adapted to suit your needs; however, the suggestions below may be helpful.

Use the **List of Assessment Sources** to keep track of the sources that you are currently using. As you plan your assessment, aim for the balance of techniques that will meet your students' needs.

On the **Individual Profile of Progress,** copy the Learning Goals from the Review and Assessment Lesson at the end of each unit. (See the *Teacher's Lesson Guide.*) Then make as many copies of the form as you need for each student in your class. Keep track of student progress on unit skills and concepts using this form. Check whether each student is Beginning, Developing, or Secure in each of the content areas. You may alternatively wish to use the **Class Checklist.**

Make several copies of the **Class Progress Indicator.** Use one page for each mathematical topic being assessed. Fill in the topic you wish to assess under the chart heading, and then write each student's name in the appropriate box, indicating whether he or she is Beginning, Developing, or Secure.

All of the other forms are to be passed out to students. Use the **interest inventories** to find out how students feel about mathematics. Their frank responses can be a useful planning tool for you. The **math log** forms can also provide insight into how comfortable students feel with the math content and, therefore, may also be useful planning tools. There are three versions of **math logs** provided: a Weekly Math Log, a generic all-purpose Math Log, and a more specific Number-Story Math Log. The **self-assessment** forms (Sample Math Work and Discussion of My Math Work) should be used as attachments to portfolio items. After students have chosen the work they wish to include in their portfolios, have them reflect on their choices, using these forms.

Name _____ Date _____ Time _____

Unit 1 Checking Progress (cont.)

Use the graph to answer Questions 5–8.

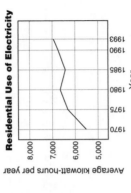

Residential Use of Electricity

Source: Commonwealth Edison

5. By about how many kilowatt-hours did residential electricity use increase from 1970 to 1993?

About __1,500__ kilowatt-hours

6. In which year was the use of electricity at its highest? __1993__

7. In which 5-year period did the amount of electricity use drop? __1980–1985__

8. During which of the following periods was the increase in the use of electricity the greatest? Circle the best answer.

(1970-1975)   1975-1980   1980-1985   1985-1990

9. Sheila got the following scores on her last 5 spelling tests:

90%   85%   92%   60%   90%

When she computed the mean, she got 95%. Explain why that answer cannot be correct. __Sample answer: The mean cannot be higher than the highest score, which is 92%.__

What is the correct mean? __83.4%__

388   Use with Lesson 1.12.

© 2002 Everyday Learning Corporation

Name _____ Date _____ Time _____

Unit 1 Checking Progress

1. Put an X next to the description that best fits the data shown in the line plot below.

__X__ The number of completed free throws out of 10 tries by each sixth grade student

____ The number of goals scored by players during a soccer game

____ The number of completed free throws out of 10 tries by each WNBA player

Explain your reasoning. __Sample answer: There are too many goals for one soccer game; and the number of completed free throws seems too low for a professional basketball player. I figured it must be free throws completed by students.__

2. What are the following landmarks for the data set above?

a. maximum __8__   **b.** minimum __0__   **c.** range __8__

d. mode(s) __3__   **e.** median __3__

3. If you wanted to find the mean for the data set above, what would you do? __Sample answer: Add the number of shots completed by each student; divide by the total number of students.__

4. The circle graph at the right shows the results of a recent survey of 3,000 adult Americans. It shows what percent of the day, on average, they spend on various activities. Use the Percent Circle to find the approximate percent for each activity, and record it on or next to the graph.

Daily Activities

- other 18%
- sleep 30%
- work 20%
- entertainment 18%
- eating & shopping 9%
- housework 5%

387

Use with Lesson 1.12.

© 2002 Everyday Learning Corporation

© 2002 Everyday Learning Corporation

Name   Date   Time

Unit 1 Checking Progress (cont.)

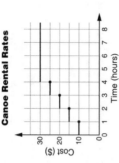

Chuck's Canoe Rental has the following rates: $10 for the first hour or fraction of an hour; $5 for each additional hour or fraction of an hour; $30 for the entire day. These rates are shown in the following step graph.

Canoe Rental Rates

(step graph: Cost ($) on vertical axis marked 10, 20, 30; Time (hours) on horizontal axis marked 0 1 2 3 4 5 6 7 8)

15. How much would it cost to rent a canoe for $1\frac{1}{2}$ hours?   **$15**

16. For 3 hours?   **$20**

17. For 3 hours and 5 minutes?   **$25**

18. Jim and his friends rent a canoe at 3:15 P.M. They don't want to pay more than 20 dollars. By what time do they need to have the canoe back?
   6:15 P.M.

19. Mr. and Mrs. Bates had their canoe out for 5 hours. Mr. Robb had his canoe out for 8 hours. Both paid the same amount of money. Why is this?
Sample answer: The rate for 5 hours is the same as the daily rate.

Use with Lesson 1.12.

Name   Date   Time

Unit 1 Checking Progress (cont.)

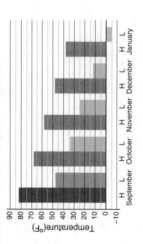

Mr. Corbeto's class kept a record of the highest and lowest temperatures in each of five months.

Monthly Highest and Lowest Temperatures (°F)

	Sept	Oct	Nov	Dec	Jan
Highest	82	68	58	48	38
Lowest	48	34	25	12	−5
Range	34	34	33	36	43

10. Complete the bar graph to the right showing the highest and lowest temperatures for each of the five months. Then use the table and the graph to answer the questions that follow.

(bar graph: Temperature (°F) vertical axis from −10 to 90; horizontal axis showing H L for September, October, November, December, January)

11. What was the lowest temperature recorded during the five months?   **−5°F**

12. What was the range between the highest and lowest temperatures for September?   **34°F**

13. a. Which month had the greatest range between the highest and lowest temperatures?   **January**

   b. What was that range?   **43°F**

14. One of Mr. Corbeto's students said, "This graph shows that most days in September are in the 80s, while most nights are in the 40s." Explain why you agree or disagree with this statement.
Sample answer: I disagree because the graph does not give information about day and night temperatures.

Use with Lesson 1.12.

© 2002 Everyday Learning Corporation

Name _____ Date _____ Time _____

Unit 2 Checking Progress (cont.)

Add or subtract.

18. $0.394 + 5.62 =$ __6.014__

19. __21.69__ $= 17.6 + 4.09$

20. __7.67__ $= 8.07 - 0.4$

21. $7.4 - 3.82 =$ __3.58__

Multiply.

22. $4.9 * 6.8 =$ __33.32__

23. $72.3 * 5.6 =$ __404.88__

24. __3.22__ $= 0.35 * 9.2$

25. __2.73__ $= 13 * 0.21$

Use with Lesson 2.12.

© 2002 Everyday Learning Corporation

392

Name _____ Date _____ Time _____

Unit 2 Checking Progress

Compare each pair of numbers. Write <, >, or =.

1. 5 hundredths __>__ 0.0005

2. 75 thousandths __=__ 0.075

3. 1,005,000 __<__ 1.5 million

4. $2.5 * 10^3$ __<__ 25,000

5. $1.2 * 10^6$ __=__ 1.2 million

6. $\frac{1}{100}$ __>__ 0.0001

Write each number in standard notation.

7. 4.6 million __4,600,000__

8. 32.1 trillion __32,100,000,000,000__

Write each number in number-and-word notation.

9. 5,600,000,000 __5.6 billion__

10. 462,800,000,000,000 __462.8 trillion__

Write the exponent in each of the following.

11. $10 * 10 * 10 * 10 = 10^{\boxed{4}}$

12. $0.0001 = 10^{\boxed{-4}}$

13. $1 \text{ billion} = 10^{\boxed{9}}$

14. $\frac{1}{10} = 10^{\boxed{-1}}$

15. $0.1 * 0.1 * 0.1 = 10^{\boxed{-3}}$

16. $3 * 3 * 3 * 3 * 3 = 3^{\boxed{5}}$

17. Which is greater, 7^2 or 2^7? $\boxed{2^7}$
Show or explain how you got your answer.
__Sample answer: I entered each one into the calculator__
__to find the answer. $7^2 = 49$ and $2^7 = 128$.__

Use with Lesson 2.12.

© 2002 Everyday Learning Corporation

391

Unit 2 Checking Progress (cont.)

Name   Date   Time

Divide.

26. 180 / 15 = __12__

27. 990 / 38 → __26 R2__

28. 1,064 / 46 → __23 R6__

29. 37.94 / 7 = __5.42__

30. 15.8 / 20 = __0.79__

31. Give the answer to two decimal places: 89 / 43 = __2.06, or 2.07__

Unit 3 Checking Progress

Name   Date   Time

1. Give two special cases for the general pattern $m + m + k = (2 * m) + k$.

Sample answers: $4 + 4 + 5 = (2 * 4) + 5$

$\frac{1}{2} + \frac{1}{2} + 6 = (2 * \frac{1}{2}) + 6$

2. Circle all of the statements below that describe the special cases at the right.

$2 * 7 = 7 + 7$
$2 * 1.5 = 1.5 + 1.5$
$2 * 0 = 0 + 0$

a. Doubling a number is the same as adding it to itself.

b. $2 * n = 2 + 2$ **c.** $2 * a = b + c$

d. (circled) $2 * a = a + a$

Refer to the picture at the right. Write an algebraic expression that describes each of the following situations.

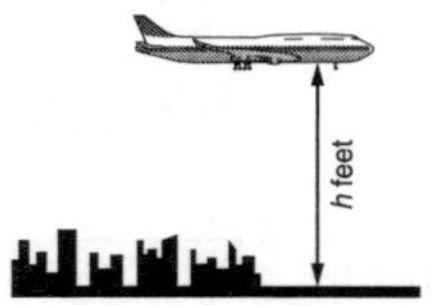

h feet

3. The height of the plane if it climbs 2,000 feet higher $h + 2,000$

4. The height of the plane if it descends 1,500 feet $h - 1,500$

5. The height of another plane 7 feet above this plane $h + 7$

Mr. Dini used the spreadsheet at the right to record his students' scores on three spelling tests. Column E shows their mean (average) scores.

	A	B	C	D	E
1	Student	Test 1	Test 2	Test 3	Mean
2	Cheri	100	100	100	100
3	Sam	50	80	74	68
4	Dave	100	95	95	97
5	Jenna	80	100	90	90

6. What score did Sam receive on Test 2? __80__

7. What is shown in Cell C4? __95__

8. Calculate Jenna's mean score and write it in Cell E5. __90__

9. Write a formula for calculating E5 that uses cell names. $E5 = (B5 + C5 + D5) \div 3$

Unit 3 Checking Progress (cont.)

Name Date Time

16. Complete the table for the given rule. Then plot the points and connect them to make a line graph.

Rule: $y = (\frac{1}{2} \text{ of } x) + 1$

x	y
0	1
1	$1\frac{1}{2}$
2	2
4	3
8	5

17. Eliana and Anne dropped a tennis ball, a bowling ball, and a Superball™ onto the sidewalk from a height of 3 feet. They made graphs showing the number of times the balls bounced and the heights to which they bounced. Label the graphs below with the most appropriate ball names.

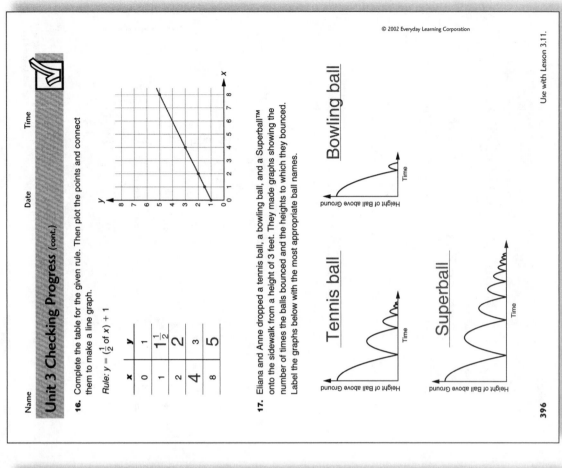

Tennis ball

Bowling ball

Superball

© 2002 Everyday Learning Corporation

Use with Lesson 3.11.

396

Unit 3 Checking Progress (cont.)

Name Date Time

10. Find the area and the perimeter of each rectangle below.

Area of a rectangle
$A = l * w$

Perimeter of a rectangle
$P = 2 * (l + w)$

a. (5 cm by 3 cm)

Area 15 cm² (unit) Perimeter 16 cm (unit)

b. (3.2 cm by 1.5 cm)

Area 4.8 cm² (unit) Perimeter 9.4 cm (unit)

11. A rectangle has a length of 4 centimeters and a width of w centimeters. What is its area? 4 * w cm² (unit)

12. Suppose the width of the rectangle in Problem 11 is 9 centimeters. What is its area? 36 cm² (unit)

The formula below can be used to find length in centimeters when length in inches is known. C is the number of centimeters, and i is the number of inches.

$$C = 2.54 * i$$

13. How many centimeters are there in 2 inches? 5.08 cm (unit)

14. How many centimeters are there in 100 inches? 254 cm (unit)

15. Circle the best approximation for the number of centimeters in 1 foot.

0.3   3.0   ⃝30   300

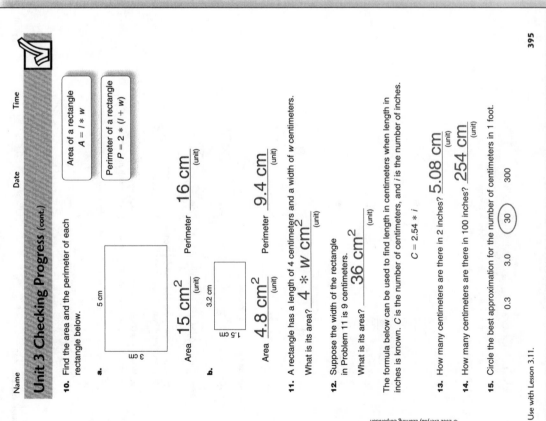

© 2002 Everyday Learning Corporation

Use with Lesson 3.11.

395

Unit 4 Checking Progress

Name   Date   Time

Write each of the following in simplest form. If possible, write each as a mixed number or whole number.

1. $\frac{8}{6} =$ $1\frac{1}{3}$
2. $\frac{18}{20} =$ $\frac{9}{10}$
3. $2\frac{6}{10} =$ $2\frac{3}{5}$
4. $\frac{42}{8} =$ $5\frac{1}{4}$

Rename each as a fraction or mixed number.
5. $15\% =$ $\frac{3}{20}$
6. $70\% =$ $\frac{7}{10}$
7. $0.8 =$ $\frac{4}{5}$
8. $1.1 =$ $1\frac{1}{10}$

Rename each as a decimal.
9. $1\frac{1}{2} =$ 1.5
10. $\frac{1}{5} =$ 0.2
11. $32\% =$ 0.32
12. $78\% =$ 0.78

Rename each as a percent.
13. $0.09 =$ 9%
14. $2.46 =$ 246%
15. $\frac{3}{5} =$ 60%
16. $\frac{99}{100} =$ 99%

17. Dallas drew a line segment $2\frac{3}{4}$ inches long. If he extends it another $\frac{3}{8}$ inch, how long will the new line segment be? $3\frac{1}{8}$ in.

18. When she began first grade, Monica was $45\frac{3}{4}$ inches tall. At the end of the year, she was $47\frac{3}{8}$ inches tall. How much had she grown? $1\frac{5}{8}$ in.

19. Juan mixed $\frac{1}{2}$ cup of whole-wheat flour with $\frac{3}{4}$ cup of white flour.
 a. How much flour is that? $1\frac{1}{4}$ cups
 b. Juan's recipe calls for 2 cups of flour. How much more flour does he need? $\frac{3}{4}$ cup more

© 2002 Everyday Learning Corporation

Use with Lesson 4.12.

Unit 4 Checking Progress (cont.)

Name   Date   Time

20. Is $\frac{7}{12}$ greater than or less than $\frac{1}{2}$?   Greater than $\frac{1}{2}$

Explain your reasoning.
Sample answer: 6 is half of 12 and 7 is more than 6; so $\frac{7}{12}$ must be more than $\frac{1}{2}$.

21. Is $\frac{7}{9} + \frac{8}{13}$ greater than or less than 1?   Greater than 1

Explain your reasoning.
Sample answer: Both $\frac{7}{9}$ and $\frac{8}{13}$ are more than $\frac{1}{2}$, so together they are greater than 1.

Add or subtract. Write all answers greater than 1 as mixed numbers. Write all answers in simplest form.

22. $\frac{3}{4} - \frac{1}{4} =$ $\frac{1}{2}$
23. $\frac{2}{3} + \frac{2}{3} =$ $1\frac{1}{3}$
24. $\frac{4}{9} + \frac{1}{3} =$ $\frac{7}{9}$
25. $\frac{9}{10} - \frac{3}{5} =$ $\frac{3}{10}$
26. $2\frac{3}{7} + 1\frac{4}{17} =$ 4
27. $3\frac{5}{6} - 2\frac{1}{6} =$ $1\frac{2}{3}$
28. $4\frac{1}{3} - 1\frac{2}{3} =$ $2\frac{2}{3}$
29. $3 - 1\frac{1}{4} =$ $1\frac{3}{4}$
30. $2\frac{1}{2} + 1\frac{1}{4} =$ $3\frac{3}{4}$
31. $2\frac{1}{8} + 1\frac{1}{16} + 1\frac{7}{8} =$ $5\frac{1}{16}$
32. $2\frac{7}{8} - 1\frac{1}{4} =$ $1\frac{5}{8}$
33. $3\frac{1}{5} - 1\frac{7}{10} =$ $1\frac{1}{2}$

© 2002 Everyday Learning Corporation

Use with Lesson 4.12.

Unit 5 Checking Progress

© 2002 Everyday Learning Corporation

Measure each angle to the nearest degree.

1.

m ∠D = __55°__

2.

m ∠T = __135°__

3. This is a reflex angle.

m ∠Q = __302°__

Draw the following angles.

4. 110° angle

5. 23° angle

6. Draw a triangle congruent to triangle *DEN*. Line segment *PR* is one of the sides of the new triangle. Label the third vertex of the triangle with the letter *A*.

Write an ordered number pair for each vertex of the new triangle.

P: (__−3__ , __1__)

A: (__0__ , __−4__)

R: (__1__ , __−1__)

Use with Lesson 5.11.

Unit 4 Checking Progress (cont.)

Solve. Write each answer in simplest form. If possible, write answers as mixed numbers or whole numbers.

34. $\frac{1}{2}$ of 48 = __24__

35. $\frac{1}{2}$ of $\frac{1}{3}$ = __$\frac{1}{6}$__

36. $\frac{1}{2} * 3\frac{1}{4}$ = __$1\frac{5}{8}$__

37. $\frac{2}{3}$ of 18 = __12__

38. $\frac{3}{4} * \frac{1}{3}$ = __$\frac{1}{4}$__

39. $3\frac{1}{2} * 2\frac{3}{8}$ = __$8\frac{5}{16}$__

40. Use a calculator to complete the table below. Then use the Percent Circle on the Geometry Template to draw a circle graph to display the data.

A survey asked students ages 8 to 18 the following question: *If you were stranded on a desert island and could choose only one of the things listed below to have with you, which would you choose?*

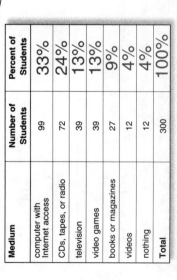

Medium	Number of Students	Percent of Students
computer with Internet access	99	33%
CDs, tapes, or radio	72	24%
television	39	13%
video games	39	13%
books or magazines	27	9%
videos	12	4%
nothing	12	4%
Total	300	100%

© 2002 Everyday Learning Corporation

Use with Lesson 4.12.

Name _____ Date _____ Time _____

Unit 5 Checking Progress (cont.)

Find the measure of each of the following angles. Do *not* use a protractor.

7. ∠a is a right angle.

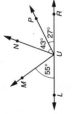

m∠a = __90°__   m∠b = __50°__

8. ∠LUR is a straight angle.

m∠MUN = __55°__

9. These two horizontal lines are parallel.

m∠c = __65°__   m∠d = __65°__

10. This is a parallelogram.

m∠e = __115°__   m∠f = __65°__

11. Quadrilateral ABCD is a parallelogram. Angles x and y have the same degree measure. What is the measure of ∠ABE? __110°__

12. Angles a and b have the same degree measure. Angles d and e have the same degree measure. What is the measure of ∠d? __35°__

© 2002 Everyday Learning Corporation

401

© 2002 Everyday Learning Corporation

Name _____ Date _____ Time _____

Unit 5 Checking Progress (cont.)

13. According to a recent survey, 15% of people between the ages of 35 and 49 have tried in-line skating. Complete the table below. Then use a protractor to make a circle graph to display the information in the table. Write a title for the graph.

	Percent of 35- to 49-Year-Olds	Degree Measure of Sector
Have tried it	15%	54°
Have not tried it	85%	306°

In-line Skating

14. Two of the sides of a kite are shown below. Using only a compass and straightedge, construct the other two sides of the kite. Look up the definition of kite in the *Student Reference Book* if you don't remember what a kite is.

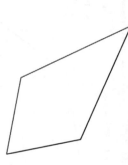

402

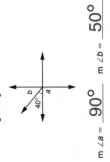

Unit 6 Checking Progress

1. Circle the number sentences below that are true.

3 = 5　　(24 * 18 = 18 * 24)　　(324 > 15)　　(One hundred twenty is twice sixty)

(a * 1 = a)　　b - 1 = b　　(67 * 18) + 54 = (54 + 18) * 67

((92 * 11) * 14 = 92 * (11 * 14))　　25 + 3 =

Write >, <, or = to complete each number sentence.

2. 54 $\underline{>}$ -58

3. -25 $\underline{>}$ -47

4. -16 $\underline{<}$ 5 + (-20)

5. -18 - (-26) $\underline{=}$ 50 + (-42)

6. -34 + (-15) $\underline{<}$ 17 - 60

7. 15 * (-20) $\underline{<}$ $\frac{2}{3}$ - $\frac{6}{9}$

8. $\frac{2}{5}$ + $\frac{3}{10}$ $\underline{<}$ 1

9. $\frac{6}{8}$ - $\frac{4}{12}$ $\underline{>}$ $\frac{2}{3}$ - $\frac{6}{9}$

Solve.

10. 24 * (-11) = $\underline{-264}$

11. $\underline{360}$ = -30 * (-12)

12. (13 + 12) * (-6) = $\underline{-150}$

13. $\underline{-59}$ = 13 + 12 * (-6)

14. -3 * (8 * 5) = $\underline{-120}$

15. $\underline{120}$ = (-3 * 8) * (-5)

16. 28 ÷ (-7) = $\underline{-4}$

17. $\underline{29}$ = 25 + (-36) ÷ (-9)

18. (OPP)(5) + (OPP)(-24) = $\underline{19}$

19. $\underline{-16}$ = (OPP)(OPP)(-8) + (-8)

20. $-\left(\frac{3}{4}\right) - \left(\frac{1}{4}\right)$ = $\underline{-1}$

21. $\frac{2}{3} \div \frac{1}{3}$ = $\underline{2}$

22. $3\frac{1}{4} \div 4$ = $\underline{\frac{13}{16}}$

23. $\frac{3}{4} * \frac{4}{3}$ = $\underline{1}$

24. $1\frac{1}{4} \div \frac{1}{2}$ = $\underline{2\frac{1}{2}}$

25. $\frac{1}{5} * -5$ = $\underline{-1}$

26. $6\frac{5}{8} - 3\frac{3}{4}$ = $\underline{2\frac{7}{8}}$

27. $\underline{2\frac{1}{2}}$ = $1\frac{5}{16} + \frac{2}{3}$

28. $5 \div \frac{2}{3}$ = $\underline{7\frac{1}{2}}$

29. $2\frac{3}{4} * \frac{2}{3}$ = $\underline{1\frac{5}{6}}$

30. Explain how solving Problem 14 can help you solve Problem 15.

Sample answer: Once you have the answer to Problem 14, all you have to do is look at the number of negative signs in Problem 15 to see that the answer is merely the opposite.

Use with Lesson 6.13.

© 2002 Everyday Learning Corporation

403

Unit 6 Checking Progress (cont.)

Insert parentheses to make each number sentence true.

31. 5 * (4 + 1) = 25

32. 4 * 8 > 50 - (2 * 10)

33. -14 * (3 - 4) > 10

34. 4 ÷ (2 + 2) ≤ (1 + 3)/4　　or　4 ÷ (2 + 2) ≤ 1 + (3/4)

Solve. Follow the rules for the order of operations.

35. 14 - 6 * 2 = $\underline{2}$

36. 3 * 13 - 16/2 = $\underline{31}$

37. $-4 * 10^2 + 6/2 + 9$ = $\underline{-388}$

38. $\left(\frac{4}{2} + 5\right)^2 + \left(\frac{6}{2} - 3\right)^3$ = $\underline{49}$

Solve the pan-balance problems.

39. 1 ball = $\underline{2}$ cubes

40. 1 glass = $\underline{5}$ spoons

41. 1 whole apple = $\underline{14}$ grapes

42. $x + x + 2 = x + 7$; $x = \underline{5}$

Find the solution for each equation.

43. (m + 25 = 53)　$m = \underline{28}$

44. 36 / s + 9 = 15　$s = \underline{6}$

45. $400 = 10^2 + y$　$y = \underline{300}$

46. (x / 2 + 7 = 21)　$x = \underline{28}$

47. Circle the two equations above that are equivalent.

Use with Lesson 6.13.

404

Assessment Masters

Page 405

Name | Date | Time

Unit 6 Checking Progress *(cont.)*

48. Millie has $2\frac{1}{4}$ cups of flour. Her recipe for one batch of cookies calls for $\frac{3}{4}$ cup of flour. How many batches of cookies can she make? Circle the equation you would use to solve the problem.

$2\frac{1}{4} * \frac{3}{4} = x$ $2\frac{1}{4} - \frac{3}{4} = x$ $\frac{3}{4} \div 2\frac{1}{4} = x$

$\boxed{2\frac{1}{4} \div \frac{3}{4} = x}$

Solve each equation.

49. $x + 5 = 27$

Operation

S 5 $x = 22$

Solution $x = 22$

50. $(\frac{1}{2})b - 6 = 32$

Operation

A 6 $(\frac{1}{2})b = 38$

D $(\frac{1}{2})$ $b = 76$

Solution $b = 76$

51. $(y - 6) + 3 = -11 + 2y$

Operation

S y $-6 + 3 = -11 + y$

S 3 $-6 = -14 + y$

A 14 $8 = y$

Solution $y = 8$

52. $3x + 18 = 39 - 4x$

Operation

S 18 $3x = 21 - 4x$

A 4x $7x = 21$

D 7 $x = 3$

Solution $x = 3$

Graph the solution set for each inequality.

53. $x > 4$

54. $x \le 4$

55. $x \ne 4$

Use with Lesson 6.13.

405

© 2002 Everyday Learning Corporation

Page 406

Name | Date | Time

Unit 7 Checking Progress

Solve.

1. $\frac{1}{2}$ of $\frac{1}{3} = \dfrac{1}{6}$

2. $\frac{2}{3}$ of $\frac{4}{5} = \dfrac{8}{15}$

3. $\frac{1}{5}$ of $\frac{2}{3} = \dfrac{2}{15}$

4. $\frac{2}{9}$ of $\frac{3}{8} = \dfrac{1}{12}$

5. $\frac{1}{3} * \frac{1}{2} = \dfrac{1}{6}$

6. $\frac{3}{2} * \frac{6}{7} = 1\dfrac{2}{7}$

7. Explain why Problems 1 and 5 have the same answer.
Sample answer: They are the same problem. They demonstrate the commutative property of multiplication, or the turn-around rule. Also, "of" means "times."

Answer the following questions about making random draws from a deck of five cards numbered 1, 2, 3, 4, and 5.

8. If you draw a card 50 times, putting the card back and mixing the deck after each draw, about how many times would you expect to draw the number 4?   10 times

9. What percent of the time would you expect to draw a 1?   20%

10. Suppose you draw the number 2. What is the probability that 2 will come up on the next draw? (Circle one.)

$\frac{1}{4}$ $\boxed{\frac{1}{5}}$ $\frac{2}{5}$

11. Explain your answer to Problem 10.
Sample answer: The cards have no memory, so the probability remains the same with each draw.

© 2002 Everyday Learning Corporation

Use with Lesson 7.9.

406

Unit 7 Checking Progress (cont.)

Name   Date   Time

12. Balls are dropped, one at a time, into the chute shown below. Each time the chute divides, the ball has an equal chance of going down any of the chutes. Sixty balls are dropped into the chute. Fill in the boxes in the tree diagram to show how many balls you would expect to go down each chute.

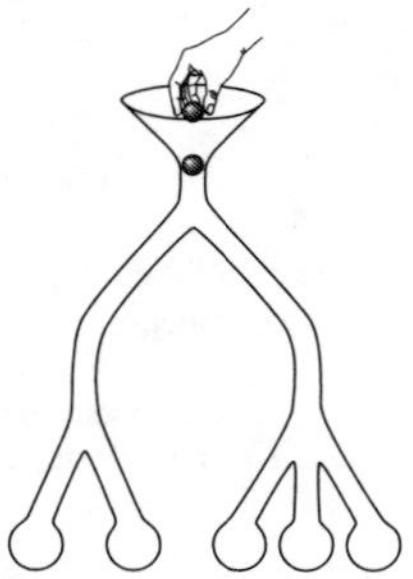

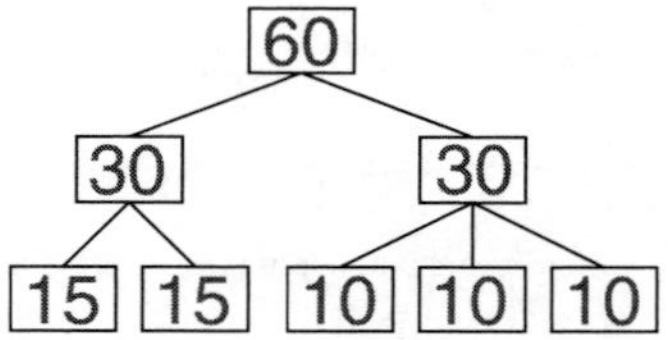

```
        60
       /  \
      30    30
     / \   / | \
    15 15 10 10 10
```

13. For each probability described below, write its letter next to the correct fraction.

a. The probability of getting HEADS when you flip a coin

b. The probability of drawing a diamond from a deck of playing cards

c. The probability of drawing the white marble from a jar with 1 white, 2 red, and 2 green marbles

d. The probability of drawing a jack from a deck of playing cards

e. The probability of getting a 4 when you roll a six-sided die

$\frac{1}{6}$ e

$\frac{1}{2}$ a

$\frac{1}{13}$ d

$\frac{1}{4}$ b

$\frac{1}{5}$ c

© 2002 Everyday Learning Corporation

407

Unit 7 Checking Progress (cont.)

Name   Date   Time

Jamie and Vern designed the game *Lucky Coin* for their school carnival. To play, flip a coin. If it lands TAILS-up, you lose. If it lands HEADS-up, you get to flip again. If it lands HEADS-up on the second flip, you win a prize. If it lands TAILS-up, you lose. Make a tree diagram to help you answer the questions below.

```
1st flip: heads ――― 1/2
                \
                 1/2 ――― tails
        1/2
2nd flip: heads ――― 1/2
         win prize  \
                     1/2 ――― tails
```

14. What is the probability of winning *Lucky Coin*?

$\frac{1}{4}$

15. If 100 people play *Lucky Coin*, how many would you expect to win?

25 people

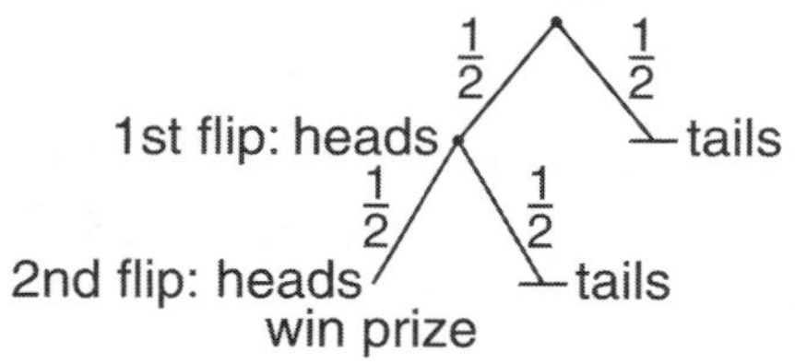

16. Explain why this is not a fair game.

Sample answer: The chances of winning and losing are not equal.

17. How would you change the rules to make *Lucky Coin* a fair game?

Sample answer: Flip a coin twice. If it lands on the same side both times, you win.

© 2002 Everyday Learning Corporation

408

Name _____ Date _____ Time _____

Unit 7 Checking Progress (cont.)

Refer to the spinner at the right. Name the color that fits each of the following statements.

18. The spinner will land on this color about as often as it lands on white. **blue**

19. The chance of getting this color is $\frac{1}{6}$. **red**

20. The probability of landing on this color is greater than 30%. **green**

21. In 6 spins, the spinner lands on red 4 times. Explain how this is possible if the spinner should only land on red 1 out of every 6 times.

Sample answer: The actual results, in a small sample of trials, is often very different from the expected probability. The more trials that are done, the closer the results will be to the expected probability.

22. In the space below, draw and label a Venn diagram showing the following information about Mr. Penn's class:
- 21 students have either a dog, a cat, or both a dog and a cat.
- 14 students have a dog.
- 4 of the students who have a dog also have a cat.

dogs   cats

How many students have a cat but no dog? **7 students**

© 2002 Everyday Learning Corporation

Use with Lesson 7.9.

409

Name _____ Date _____ Time _____

Unit 8 Checking Progress

© 2002 Everyday Learning Corporation

Refer to the advertisement on the right to solve Problems 1–4 below.

1. Complete the rate table.

inches	3	9	36	12	1
people	1	3	12	4	$\frac{1}{3}$

☞ **Feed 12 people for $18!**

You can, when you buy a **3-foot** cold-cut party submarine sandwich.

2. If 12 people share a sandwich equally, how many inches will each person get? **3 in.**

3. What is the cost per person? **$1.50**

4. Explain how you figured out the cost per person.

Sample answer: I divided 18 by 12.

Use cross multiplication to determine if the following fractions are equivalent.

5. $\frac{2}{8}$ and $\frac{3}{12}$ **yes** $8 * 3 = 24$ $2 * 12 = 24$

6. $\frac{3}{20}$ and $\frac{15}{60}$ **no** $20 * 15 = 300$ $3 * 60 = 180$

7. $\frac{9}{15}$ and $\frac{6}{10}$ **yes** $15 * 6 = 90$ $9 * 10 = 90$

Use cross multiplication to solve the proportions below.

8. $\frac{4}{10} = \frac{10}{m}$ $m = 25$

9. $\frac{12}{f} = \frac{8}{12}$ $f = 18$

10. $\frac{g}{20} = \frac{4}{16}$ $g = 5$

11. $\frac{4}{6} = \frac{k}{15}$ $k = 10$

Use with Lesson 8.13.

410

Name _____ Date _____ Time _____

Unit 8 Checking Progress (cont.)

For each problem below, complete the corresponding rate table. Use the table to write an open proportion. Solve the proportion. Write the answer to the problem.

12. Some species of bamboo grow at a rate of 3 inches every 6 hours. About how many hours does it take to grow 4 inches? __8 hours__

inches	1	3	4	6	$\frac{1}{2}$
hours	2	6	8	12	1

$$\frac{3}{6} = \frac{4}{n}$$

13. Mr. Macaroni rode his motorcycle 120 miles on 3 gallons of gasoline. How far can he ride on 4.5 gallons? __180 miles__

miles	1	120	40	180
gallons	0.025	3	1	4.5

$$\frac{120}{3} = \frac{n}{4.5}$$

Write proportions to solve the problems below.

14. Jennie bought 6 boxes of pencils for $4. How many boxes of pencils can she buy with $6?

$$\frac{boxes}{dollars} = \frac{6}{4} = \frac{n}{6}$$

Answer __9 boxes__

15. George was reading a mystery story. He read 40 pages in 60 minutes. How many pages did he read in 40 minutes?

$$\frac{pages}{minutes} = \frac{40}{60} = \frac{n}{40}$$

Answer __About 27 pages__

16. Shawn missed 40% of the questions on the last science test. How many questions did he miss if there were 20 questions on the test?

$$\frac{questions\ missed}{number\ of\ questions} = \frac{40}{100} = \frac{n}{20}$$

Answer __8 questions__

17. Melinda went to bat 48 times last season. She had 16 hits. What percent of the time did she make a hit?

$$\frac{hits}{times\ at\ bat} = \frac{16}{48} = \frac{n}{100}$$

Answer __$33\frac{1}{3}$%__

© 2002 Everyday Learning Corporation

Name _____ Date _____ Time _____

Unit 8 Checking Progress (cont.)

18. The table below shows the calorie and fat content in 1 cup of two kinds of yogurt. Complete the table.

Food Label	Food	Calories from Fat / Total Calories	Estimated Fat Percent
Nutrition Facts Serving Size 1 cup (225 g) Servings Per Container 1 Amount Per Serving Calories 260 Calories from Fat 73	strawberry yogurt	$\frac{73}{260}$	About 28%
Nutrition Facts Serving Size 1 cup (225 g) Servings Per Container 1 Amount Per Serving Calories 220 Calories from Fat 42	vanilla yogurt	$\frac{42}{220}$	About 19%

19. Explain how you estimated the percent of fat for vanilla yogurt.
__Answers vary.__

20. Three out of every 5 cards are faceup. If 20 cards are facedown, how many cards are there in all? __50 cards__

21. The ratio of facedown to faceup cards is 2 to 3. If there are 25 cards altogether, how many cards are facedown? __10 cards__

22. Shade $\frac{4}{5}$ of the circles below.

23. What percent of the circles is shaded? __80%__

24. What is the ratio of shaded circles to unshaded circles? __8 to 2, or 8:2__

25. How many more unshaded circles would you have to draw so that the ratio of shaded circles to unshaded circles would be 2 to 1? __2 more circles__

Name   Date   Time

Unit 8 Checking Progress (cont.)

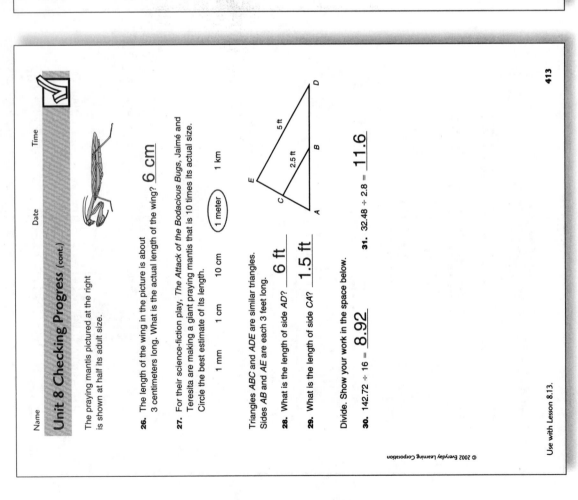

The praying mantis pictured at the right is shown at half its adult size.

26. The length of the wing in the picture is about 3 centimeters long. What is the actual length of the wing? __6 cm__

27. For their science-fiction play, *The Attack of the Bodacious Bugs*, Jaimé and Teresita are making a giant praying mantis that is 10 times its actual size. Circle the best estimate of its length.

1 mm   1 cm   10 cm   (1 meter)   1 km

Triangles *ABC* and *ADE* are similar triangles. Sides *AB* and *AE* are each 3 feet long.

28. What is the length of side *AD*? __6 ft__

29. What is the length of side *CA*? __1.5 ft__

Divide. Show your work in the space below.

30. $142.72 \div 16 =$ __8.92__

31. $32.48 \div 2.8 =$ __11.6__

© 2002 Everyday Learning Corporation

Use with Lesson 8.13.

413

Name   Date   Time

Unit 9 Checking Progress

1. Each of the following expressions describes the area of one of the rectangles below. Write the letter of the rectangle next to the expression.

a. $6 * (5 + 7)$ __A__   **b.** $(7 + 6) * 5$ __B__

c. $30 + 35$ __B__   **d.** $(5 * 6) + (7 * 6)$ __A__

Rectangle A

Rectangle B

2. a. What is the area of the rectangle at the right? __30__ units²

b. What is the area of the shaded part of the rectangle? __18__ units²

3. Use the formula $A = \pi * r^2$ to find the area of the circle at the right. Write your answer to the nearest square centimeter.

__28 cm²__

4. Explain how you got your answer to Problem 3. __Sample answer: I substituted 3 for the *r* in the formula and then solved for the area.__

© 2002 Everyday Learning Corporation

Use with Lesson 9.14.

414

Unit 9 Checking Progress (cont.)

Use the formulas to solve the problems below. Record the formula you use to solve the problem. (You may need to use more than one formula.) Then solve the problem.

Area
$A = b * h$ (rectangle, parallelogram)
$A = \frac{1}{2} * b * h$ (triangle)
$A = \pi r^2$ (circle)
Circumference $C = \pi d$, or $C = 2\pi r$

Volume
$V = B * h$, or $l * w * h$ (rectangular prism)
$V = B * h$, or $\pi * r^2 * h$ (cylinder)
$V = \frac{4}{3} * \pi * r^3$ (sphere)
Pythagorean Theorem $a^2 + b^2 = c^2$

17.

Formula $A = \frac{1}{2} * b * h$

Area 54 cm^2

18.

Formula $A = \pi r^2$

Area 78.5 cm^2

19.

Formula $V = B * h$, or $\pi * r^2 * h$

Volume 381.5 cm^3

20.

Formula $V = B * h$, or $l * w * h$

Volume 180 in.^{3}

21.

Formula $A = b * h$

Area 63 in.^{2}

22.

Formula $a^2 + b^2 = c^2$

$c = $ 10 ft

23. The perimeter of Triangle *CRY* is 20 meters. Find the length of each side of the triangle.

Length of $\overline{CR}$ 8 m   Length of $\overline{RY}$ 8 m

Length of $\overline{CY}$ 4 m

416

Use with Lesson 9.14.

© 2002 Everyday Learning Corporation

Unit 9 Checking Progress (cont.)

Simplify each expression.

5. $n + 2n + 3n = $ $6n$

6. $4c - 7c = $ $-3c$

7. $5 + 12x - 16 - 8x = $ $4x - 11$

8. $e + 19 + 4(e - 2) = $ $11 + 5e$

9. Explain how you would simplify $5(y - 2) + 6y - 6$.

Sample answer: First distribute the 5 over the expression in parentheses to get $5y - 10 + 6y - 6$. Then combine like terms to get $11y - 16$.

Solve each equation.

10. $9d - 3d = 18$

Solution $d = 3$

11. $2(x + 4) = 20$

Solution $x = 6$

12. $15 = 2 * (x - \frac{1}{2})$

Solution $x = 8$

13. $3x - 5 = 5x + 11$

Solution $x = -8$

The formula for converting Celsius temperatures to Fahrenheit is $F = (1.8 * C) + 32$.

14. If $C = -10$, what is F? 14

15. If $F = 122$, what is C? 50

16. Which formula is equivalent to $F = (1.8 * C) + 32$? (Circle one.)

$3.2F = 1.8C$ $F + 32 = 1.8C$ (F − 32 = 1.8C)

Use with Lesson 9.14.

415

© 2002 Everyday Learning Corporation

Assessment Masters

Unit 9 Checking Progress (cont.)

Name   Date   Time

Mr. Merlin is a home repairman. He charges $25 per hour and rounds his time to the nearest quarter of an hour. Below is a spreadsheet that shows a record of his last 3 jobs.

	A	B	C	D
1	Customer	Job	Hours	Charge (at $25 per hour)
2	Mrs. Martinez	Window repairs	3.5	87.50
3	Mr. O'Hara	Repair kitchen ceiling	6.25	156.25
4	Ms. Liu	Install ceiling fan	5.5	137.50

24. Circle the formula stored in Cell D2.

    C2 + C3   C2 * C3   (C2 * 25)   D4 * 25

25. Write the formula that belongs in Cell D4.   D1 * C4

26. Calculate the amount that should appear in D4 and write it in the cell.

The mobile shown is in balance.

27. The fulcrum of the mobile at the right is the center point of the rod.

    What is the weight of the object to the right of the fulcrum?   6   units

Reminder:
$(W * D) = (w * d)$

28. Find an approximate solution to the equation $x^2 + 4 = 94$. Use trial and error. Record your results in the table. A first guess is shown. Stop when you get within 1 of 94.

Sample answers:

x	x^2	$x^2 + 4$	Compare $x^2 + 4$ to 94
9	81	85	85 < 94
8	64	68	x = 8 is too small.
5	25	29	x = 5 is too small.
9.5	90.25	94.25	x = 9.5 is slightly too large.

© 2002 Everyday Learning Corporation

Unit 10 Checking Progress

Name   Date   Time

© 2002 Everyday Learning Corporation

Circle the objects that are topologically equivalent to the first item.

1.

For Problems 2–8, write true or false.

2. This design is a tessellation.   true

3. This design is *not* a tessellation.   true

4. This notation describes the tessellation. 3.6.3.6.   true

5. This notation describes the tessellation. 4.8.8.   true

Name   Date   Time

Midyear Assessment

1. Shade the circle in front of the best answer for each problem below. Show your work on the grid when necessary.

© 2002 Everyday Learning Corporation

a. $1.46 + 2.98 =$	○ 4	● 4.44	○ 44	○ 5
b. $6.9 - 0.43 =$	○ 2.6	○ 26	● 6.47	○ 6.53
c. $-13 + (20) =$	○ -33	○ -7	● 7	○ 15
d. $10^4 =$	○ 40	○ 100	● 10,000	○ 104
e. $10^{-3} =$	○ 1	○ 1,000	● 0.001	○ 0.0001
f. $2,024 \div 4 =$	○ 56	● 506	○ 508	○ not given
g. $\dfrac{6,092}{3} \rightarrow$	○ 203 R2	○ 230 R2	○ 2,032	● 2,030 R2
h. $2.3 * 5 =$	○ 10.3	○ 1.05	● 11.5	○ 115.0
i. $100 * 1.2 =$	○ 1.200	● 120.0	○ 1,200	○ 1,001.2
j. $5.1 * 3.9 =$	● 19.89	○ 1.989	○ 0.1989	○ 198.9

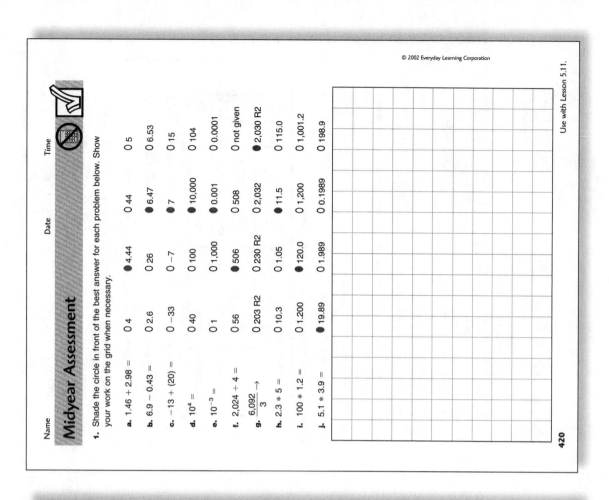

420

Use with Lesson 5.11.

Name   Date   Time

Unit 10 Checking Progress (cont.)

6. In the figure at the right, it is unlikely that you would ever be able to make a cut so that the cross section would show a square.
   <u>true</u>

7. If you sliced the figure at the right correctly, you would be able to get a cross section in the shape of a triangle.
   <u>true</u>

8. It is unlikely that you would ever be able to make a cut that would show a cross section in the shape of a circle from the figure at the right.
   <u>true</u>

9. The design below was made by beginning with a __square__ and then __sliding__ it to the right, up, and to the right.

   Then the new figure was __translated__ along a horizontal line to create interlocking pieces.

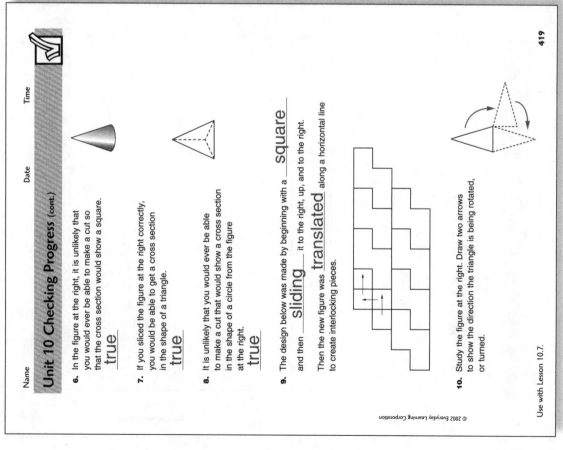

10. Study the figure at the right. Draw two arrows to show the direction the triangle is being rotated, or turned.

© 2002 Everyday Learning Corporation

Use with Lesson 10.7.

419

Name _____ Date _____ Time _____

Midyear Assessment (cont.)

2. Add or subtract. Write all answers greater than 1 as mixed numbers. Write all answers in simplest form. Show your work on the grid when necessary.

a. $3\frac{1}{5} - 1\frac{4}{5} =$ __$1\frac{2}{5}$__

b. $\frac{4}{5} + \frac{5}{6} =$ __$1\frac{19}{30}$__

c. $3\frac{6}{1}$ = $2\frac{1}{2} + \frac{2}{3}$

d. $2\frac{1}{4}$ = $7 - 4\frac{3}{4}$

3. Multiply or divide. Show your work on the grid when necessary.

a. $45 * 92 =$ __4,140__

b. __14.82__ $= 7.8 * 1.9$

c. __86.3__ $= 345.2 \div 4$

d. $\frac{352.2}{6} =$ __$\frac{58.7}{4}$__

e. $\frac{4}{5} * \frac{1}{3} =$ __$\frac{15}{35}$__

f. $2\frac{1}{2} * 1\frac{3}{4} =$ __$\frac{35}{8}$, or $4\frac{3}{8}$__

Use with Lesson 5.11.

Name _____ Date _____ Time _____

Midyear Assessment (cont.)

© 2002 Everyday Learning Corporation

4. a. The *Mouwad Splendour* is a 101.84-carat diamond. In 1990 it sold for 12.76 million dollars. Write this number in scientific notation. __$1.276 * 10^7$__

b. The distance from Earth to the Sun is about $9.3 * 10^7$ miles. Write this number in standard notation. __93,000,000__

c. An angstrom (Å) is a unit of length. It is equivalent to 0.0000001 of a millimeter. Write this number as a power of 10. __10^{-7}__

5. Gabrielle ran the 100-yard dash five times during gym class. Her times to the nearest second were: 28, 24, 19, 25, and 22.

a. What is Gabrielle's mean time, to the nearest tenth of a second? __23.6 sec__

b. What is Gabrielle's median time? __24 sec__

6. This past summer, Vivian and her sister started a lawn-mowing and landscaping business. For four months they recorded their income and expenses in the spreadsheet below. Use the spreadsheet to answer the questions that follow.

	A	B	C	D	E	F
1		May	June	July	August	Total
2	Income	$20.00	$65.50	$75.00	$55.75	$216.25
3	Expenses	$30.70	$5.15	$0.00	$5.85	$41.70

a. During which month did Vivian and her sister have the most expenses? __May__

b. What is in Cell E2? __$55.75__

c. Compute the total income and total expenses and record them in Column F.

d. If you wanted to find the average income for the four months, which formula would you use? Circle the correct answer.

$$\frac{A2 + B2 + C2}{4} \qquad \frac{A2 + B2 + C2 + D2 + E2}{5}$$

$$\boxed{\frac{B2 + C2 + D2 + E2}{4}} \qquad \frac{B2 + C2 + D2 + E2}{5}$$

422

Use with Lesson 5.11.

Midyear Assessment (cont.)

Name ___ Date ___ Time ___

7. Write an algebraic expression, using the suggested variable, to answer each of the following questions.

a. A daddy longlegs spider has 8 legs. How many legs do S daddy longlegs spiders have?

$S * 8$ ___ legs

b. Christine has d dollars. Her brother has $8 more than she has. How much money does Christine's brother have?

$d + 8$ ___ dollars

c. Bobbie's dog is Y years old. How old was the dog 8 years ago?

$Y - 8$ ___ years old

8. Complete the "What's My Rule?" table for the given formula. Then plot the points and connect them to make a broken-line graph.

Formula: $y = x + 3$

x	y
2	5
3	6
-3	0
-5	-2
-1	2

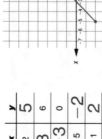

© 2002 Everyday Learning Corporation

Midyear Assessment (cont.)

Name ___ Date ___ Time ___

© 2002 Everyday Learning Corporation

9. Quadrilateral *PALE* is a parallelogram. Do not measure the angles. What is the measure of:

a. ∠ALE? 110 °

b. ∠AEL? 30 °

c. ∠PEL? 70 °

10. Find the measures of angles 1, 2, and 3. Do not measure the angles.

a. m∠1 = 60 °

b. m∠2 = 125 °

c. m∠3 = 65 °

© 2002 Everyday Learning Corporation

Name _____ Date _____ Time _____

End-of-Year Assessment

Use >, <, or = to compare the numbers.

1. 7 hundredths __>__ 0.007

2. 5,400,000 __>__ 5.2 million

3. 10^6 __>__ 100,000

4. 3^3 __<__ 33

5. $\frac{17}{3}$ __>__ $5\frac{1}{5}$

6. 0.95 __<__ $\frac{39}{40}$

7. $-15 - (-4)$ __<__ $-10 + 10$

8. $3\frac{7}{8}$ __>__ 3.6

9. Write the 9-digit number that has a 5 in the thousandths place, a 7 in the tens place, a 3 in the hundred-thousands place, a 6 in the hundreds place, and 9s in all of the remaining places. __3 9 9 , 6 7 9 . 9 9 5__

Write this number in words. __three hundred ninety-nine thousand, six hundred seventy-nine and nine hundred ninety-five thousandths__

10. Write the number that is 3 hundredths more than your answer for Problem 9. __399,680.025__

11. Round your number from Problem 10 to the nearest ten. __399,680__

Solve. Do not use a calculator.

12. $38 * 5.4 = $ __205.2__

13. $743 \div 9 = $ __82.56__

14. $\frac{401.3}{8} = $ __50.16__

15. $25.06 + 38.74 = $ __63.8__

16. $724.9 + 30.04 = $ __754.94__

17. $203.47 - 16.25 = $ __187.22__

18. $85.1 - 34.67 = $ __50.43__

19. $-29 * -32 = $ __928__

20. $-640 / 80 = $ __-8__

21. Explain how you could solve Problem 19 using mental math. __Sample answer: You could multiply 30 ∗ 32 to get 960. Then you subtract 32 to get 928. Since a negative times a negative results in a positive product, the answer is 928.__

© 2002 Everyday Learning Corporation

Name _____ Date _____ Time _____

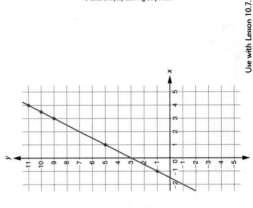

End-of-Year Assessment (cont.)

22. Explain Norma's mistake in the problem below. Then explain how to get the correct answer.

$$\frac{2}{3} \div \frac{3}{8} = \frac{1}{4}$$

__Norma multiplied the fractions to get $\frac{6}{24}$. She reduced the answer to simplest form to get $\frac{1}{4}$. She should have multiplied $\frac{2}{3}$ by the reciprocal of $\frac{3}{8}$ ($\frac{8}{3}$) to get $\frac{16}{9}$ or $1\frac{7}{9}$.__

Write an algebraic expression for each of the following.

23. Antoinette is 8 years older than her brother Darrin who is D years old.

Antoinette is __$D + 8$__ years old.

24. Jean reads three times as fast as her sister Monica who reads R pages per minute. Jean reads __$R * 3$__ pages per minute.

25. Melissa caught 5 more than twice as many fish as her brother Michael. Michael caught F fish. Melissa caught __$(F * 2) + 5$__ fish.

26. Complete the table for the given rule. Then plot the points and connect them to make a line graph.

Rule: $2x + 3 = y$

x	y
1	5
3	9
3.5	10
4	11
-1	1

© 2002 Everyday Learning Corporation

Name   Date   Time

End-of-Year Assessment (cont.)

32. Explain how you change a percent into a degree measure. Use an example.
Sample answer: There are 360° in a circle. To change
25% to a degree measure, find 25% of 360°. 0.25 * 360
$= 90$ or $\frac{1}{4} * 360 = 90.$ 25% of a circle is 90°.

33. What tool would you use to make your circle graph if the expenses
in Problem 30 were all given as degree measures? (Circle one.)

Percent Circle   Compass   (Protractor)

34. Write 5 other names for $\frac{2}{5}$. (Include a decimal and a percent.) Sample answers:

$\frac{45}{}$ ____ $\frac{6}{15}$ ____ $\frac{20}{50}$ ____

0.4 ____   40% ____ $\frac{10}{}$ ____ $\frac{2}{5}$

35. Jim has 5 playing cards. There are two aces, one queen,
one seven, and one ten. If someone picks one of Jim's
cards at random, what is the probability that it is an ace? ____

36. Draw an acute angle below.   Sample answer:

C •

T

A

Explain what an acute angle is. Sample answer: An acute angle
measures less than 90°.

37. Measure the angle you drew in Problem 36.
My angle measures about ____°. Answers vary.

Use with Lesson 10.7.

Name   Date   Time

End-of-Year Assessment (cont.)

27. Make up a number story that the rule in Problem 26 might describe.
Sample answer: Robert had $3 dollars in his savings
account. He earned $2 per week for taking out the
garbage. If he saves everything he earns, how much
money will he have after x weeks?

28. David drew a line segment that was $3\frac{1}{8}$ inches long.
If he extends it another $\frac{3}{4}$ of an inch, how long will the
new line segment be? $3\frac{7}{8}$ inches

Write a number sentence to show how you found
your answer. $3\frac{1}{8} + \frac{3}{4} = x$

29. A triangle has angles of 35° and 75°.
What is the measure of the third angle?   70°

Explain how you found your answer. Sample answer: I know that the
sum of the angles of a triangle is 180°, so I subtracted the
sum of 35 and 75 from 180 to get my answer.

30. Mr. and Mrs. Weiss's vacation expenses are shown in the table below.
Amounts are rounded to the nearest dollar.

	Gasoline	Lodging (camping and motels)	Food	Miscellaneous Expenses
Amount	$75	$320	$147	$82
Percent	12%	51%	24%	13%

What were the Weiss's total expenses for the vacation? $624

Complete the bottom row of the table showing
the percent of the total spent for each kind
of expense. Round to the nearest whole percent.

31. Use your Percent Circle to draw a circle graph
for the expenses in Problem 30.

The Weiss's Vacation Expenses

gas | misc | food | lodging

Use with Lesson 10.7.

© 2002 Everyday Learning Corporation

Name _____ Date _____ Time _____

End-of-Year Assessment (cont.)

Use cross multiplication to solve the proportions.

38. $\frac{7}{8} = \frac{s}{24}$

$s = 21$

39. $\frac{12}{m} = \frac{9}{15}$

$m = 20$

40. $\frac{6}{9} = \frac{22}{t}$

$t = 33$

41. Sid found a mysterious plant that grows very quickly. It grows at a constant rate. Complete the rate table.

Inches	2.5	5	10	12.5	25
Weeks	1	2	4	5	10

42. Explain how you found the number of inches for 10 weeks in Problem 41.

Sample answer: I know that it will grow half as much in two weeks as in four weeks, so I know that it will grow 5 inches in 2 weeks. I know that it will grow 5 times as much in ten weeks as in two weeks, so I know that it will grow 25 inches in ten weeks.

43. If $\frac{2}{3}$ of a set of cards is facedown, and there are 16 cards facedown, how many cards are there altogether? __24 cards__

Explain your answer. Sample answer: I know that two-thirds is 16, so each third is 8. Three-thirds would be 24.

© 2002 Everyday Learning Corporation

429

© 2002 Everyday Learning Corporation

Name _____ Date _____ Time _____

End-of-Year Assessment (cont.)

Solve the following equations.

44. $4 + 2 * x = 12$

Solution: $x = 4$

45. $3 * (x + 2^2) = 30$

Solution: $x = 6$

46. $5x + 2 + 3x = 18$

Solution: $x = 2$

47. $(x - 24) \div 2 = 18$

Solution: $x = 60$

48. The perimeter of this rectangle is 30 cm.

a. What is the area of the rectangle? __36__ cm²

(rectangle: $2x$ cm wide, 4 cm and 3 cm sides)

b. Describe in words or use numbers to show how you solved the problem.

Sample answer:

$Perimeter = 3 + 3 + 4 + 4 + 2x + 2x$ $Area = l * w$

$30 = 3 + 3 + 4 + 4 + 2x + 2x$ $A = (2x + 4) * 3$

$30 = 14 + 4x$ $A = ((2 * 4) + 4) * 3$

$16 = 4x$ $A = (8 + 4) * 3$

$4 = x$ $A = 12 * 3$

Use this value of x to find the area. $A = 36 \text{ cm}^2$

430

Name   Date   Time

End-of-Year Assessment (cont.)

49. If Shawn flips a fair coin 3 times, what is the probability that he will get 3 heads? $\dfrac{1}{8}$

50. Draw a tree diagram to show the probability of getting three heads in Problem 49. **Sample answer:**

1st flip:

2nd flip:

3rd flip:

51. Shawn flips a fair coin 5 times and it lands heads up each time. What is the probability that it will land tails up on the next flip? $\dfrac{1}{2}$

Explain. **Sample answer:** The probability that it will land tails up is still $\dfrac{1}{2}$ or one out of two. The coin has no memory of the past flips.

52. Without using a protractor, find the missing angle measures. Record your answers on the drawing. (Lines that appear parallel are.)

$y = 45°$; $x = 135°$; $z = 135°$

© 2002 Everyday Learning Corporation

Use with Lesson 10.7.

431

Name   Date   Time

End-of-Year Assessment (cont.)

© 2002 Everyday Learning Corporation

Use the spreadsheet below to answer Problems 53–56. Mrs. Wilson recorded her students' science test grades on a spreadsheet. The scores for two students are shown below.

	A	B	C	D	E	F
		Science Test Grades				
1	Student	Test 1	Test 2	Test 3	Test 4	Average (Mean)
2	José	92	65	90	88	83.8
3	Keisha	100	85	95	93	93.3

53. What information is in Cell B2? José's score on Test 1, or 92

54. Mrs. Wilson made an error when she recorded Keisha's score on Test 4. Keisha actually got 95% correct. Which cell(s) should be changed? E3 and F3

55. Which formula can be found in Cell F2? (Circle your answer.)

E2 ÷ 4   (B2 + C2 + D2 + E2) ÷ 4   A2 * 4   (E2 + E3) ÷ 2

56. Mrs. Wilson gave José the choice of using either his mean score or his median score for his final grade. Which would be the better choice? The median

Why? Sample answer: His median score is higher because the median is halfway between 88 and 90. The median is 89.

Use with Lesson 10.7.

432

Class Checklist: Unit 1

Copyright © SRA/McGraw-Hill

Class _____

Dates _____

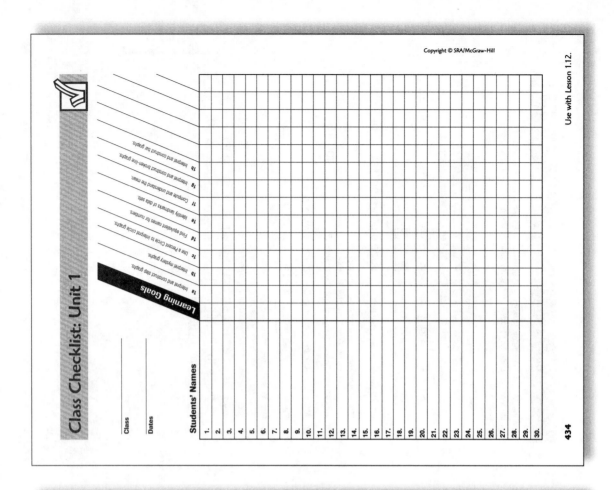

Learning Goals

1a Interpret and construct step graphs.
1b Interpret mystery graphs.
1c Use a Percent Circle to interpret circle graphs.
1d Find equivalent names for numbers.
1e Identify landmarks of data sets.
1f Compute and understand the mean.
1g Interpret and construct broken-line graphs.
1h Interpret and construct bar graphs.

Students' Names

1.
2.
3.
4.
5.
6.
7.
8.
9.
10.
11.
12.
13.
14.
15.
16.
17.
18.
19.
20.
21.
22.
23.
24.
25.
26.
27.
28.
29.
30.

Use with Lesson 1.12.

Name _____ Date _____ Time _____

End-of-Year Assessment (cont.)

57. Write the following numbers in scientific notation.

a. 2,400,000 $2.4 * 10^6$ b. 0.007 $7 * 10^{-3}$

58. The area of the triangle at the right is 12 cm².
What is the value of x? $X = 3$

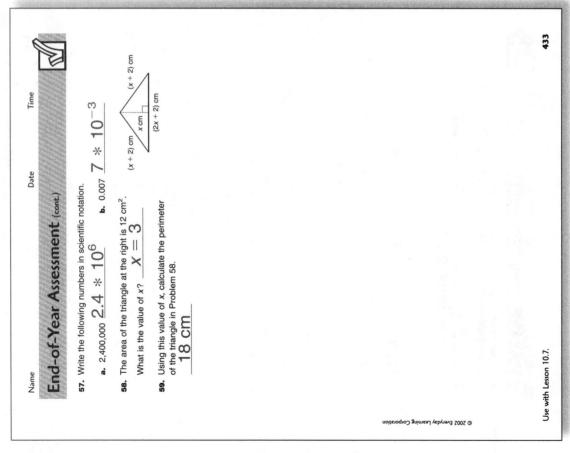

$(x + 2)$ cm

x cm

$(2x + 2)$ cm

$(x + 2)$ cm

59. Using this value of x, calculate the perimeter
of the triangle in Problem 58.
18 cm

© 2002 Everyday Learning Corporation

Use with Lesson 10.7.

© 2002 Everyday Learning Corporation

Class Checklist: Unit 2

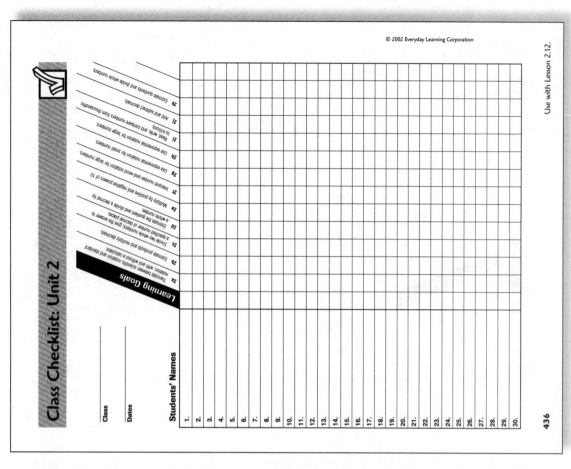

Class _____

Dates _____

Learning Goals

- 2a Translate between scientific notation and standard notation, with and without a calculator.
- 2b Estimate products and multiply decimals.
- 2c Divide two whole numbers; divide decimals.
- 2d Estimate the quotient and divide a decimal by a whole number.
- 2e Estimate the answer to a specified number of decimal places.
- 2f Multiply by positive and negative powers of 10.
- 2g Interpret number-and-word notation for large numbers.
- 2h Use exponential notation for large numbers.
- 2i Use exponential notation for small numbers.
- 2j Read, write, and compare numbers from thousandths to trillions.
- 2k Add and subtract decimals.
- 2l Estimate quotients and divide whole numbers.

Students' Names

1.
2.
3.
4.
5.
6.
7.
8.
9.
10.
11.
12.
13.
14.
15.
16.
17.
18.
19.
20.
21.
22.
23.
24.
25.
26.
27.
28.
29.
30.

Use with Lesson 2.12.

436

Student's Name _____   Date _____

Individual Profile of Progress: Unit 1

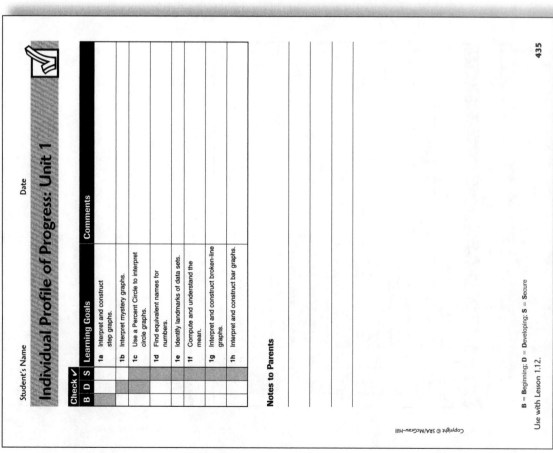

Check ✓			Learning Goals	Comments
B	**D**	**S**		
			1a Interpret and construct step graphs.	
			1b Interpret mystery graphs.	
			1c Use a Percent Circle to interpret circle graphs.	
			1d Find equivalent names for numbers.	
			1e Identify landmarks of data sets.	
			1f Compute and understand the mean.	
			1g Interpret and construct broken-line graphs.	
			1h Interpret and construct bar graphs.	

Notes to Parents

B = Beginning; **D** = Developing; **S** = Secure

Use with Lesson 1.12.

Copyright © SRA/McGraw-Hill

435

Class Checklist: Unit 3

Copyright © SRA/McGraw-Hill

Class ____

Dates ____

Learning Goals

3a	Use variables to describe general patterns.	
3b	Use a spreadsheet.	
3c	Interpret mystery graphs.	
3d	Write algebraic expressions to represent situations.	
3e	Evaluate algebraic expressions and formulas.	
3f	Mentally add 1-digit integers.	
3g	Represent rates with formulas, tables, and graphs.	
3h	Convert between fractions and mixed numbers.	
3i	Find the least common multiple of two numbers.	
3j	Find the greatest common factor of two numbers.	

Students' Names

1.
2.
3.
4.
5.
6.
7.
8.
9.
10.
11.
12.
13.
14.
15.
16.
17.
18.
19.
20.
21.
22.
23.
24.
25.
26.
27.
28.
29.
30.

Use with Lesson 3.11.

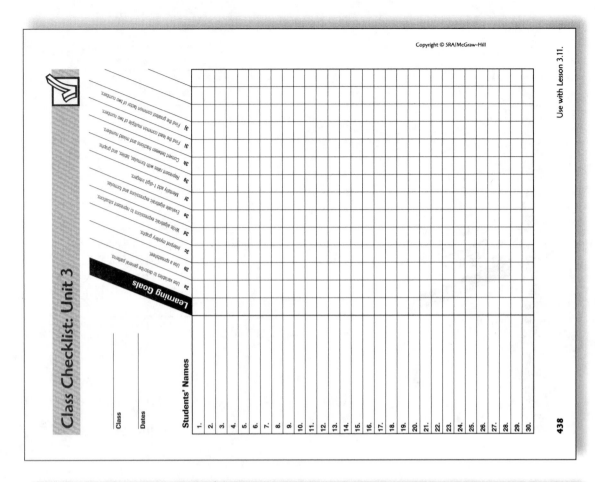

Student's Name ____   Date ____

Individual Profile of Progress: Unit 2

Check ✓			Learning Goals	Comments
B	**D**	**S**		
			2a	Translate between scientific notation and standard notation, with and without a calculator.	
			2b	Estimate products and multiply decimals.	
			2c	Divide two whole numbers; give the answer to a specified number of decimal places.	
			2d	Estimate the quotient and divide a decimal by a whole number.	
			2e	Multiply by positive and negative powers of 10.	
			2f	Interpret number-and-word notation for large numbers.	
			2g	Use exponential notation for small numbers.	
			2h	Use exponential notation for large numbers.	
			2i	Read, write, and compare numbers from thousandths to trillions.	
			2j	Add and subtract decimals.	
			2k	Estimate quotients and divide whole numbers.	

Notes to Parents

B = Beginning; **D** = Developing; **S** = Secure

Use with Lesson 2.12.

Copyright © SRA/McGraw-Hill

Class Checklist: Unit 4

Class _____

Dates _____

Learning Goals

4a Construct circle graphs with the Percent Circle.
4b Use circle graphs to interpret data.
4c Use an algorithm to multiply fractions and mixed numbers.
4d Use an algorithm to add and subtract mixed numbers having fractions with unlike denominators.
4e Use an algorithm to subtract mixed numbers having fractions with like denominators.
4f Find a percent of a number.
4g Use an algorithm to add mixed numbers having fractions with like denominators.
4h Use an algorithm to add and subtract fractions with like and unlike denominators.
4i Compare and order fractions.
4j Convert between fractions, mixed numbers, decimals, and percents.
4k Write fractions and mixed numbers in simplest form.

Students' Names

1.
2.
3.
4.
5.
6.
7.
8.
9.
10.
11.
12.
13.
14.
15.
16.
17.
18.
19.
20.
21.
22.
23.
24.
25.
26.
27.
28.
29.
30.

Copyright © SRA/McGraw-Hill

Use with Lesson 4.12.

440

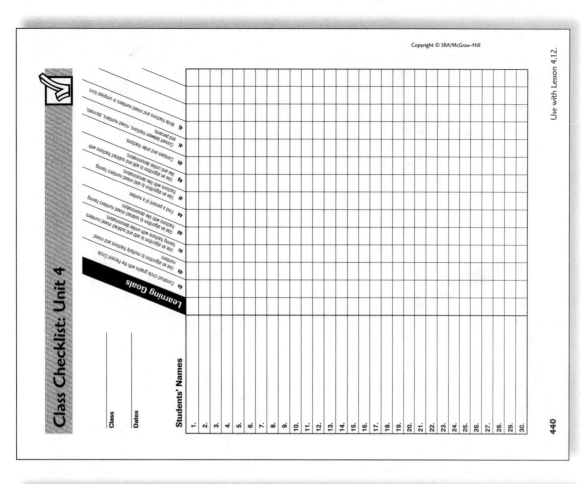

Student's Name _____   Date _____

Individual Profile of Progress: Unit 3

Check ✔			Learning Goals	Comments
B	**D**	**S**		
			3a Use variables to describe general patterns.	
			3b Use a spreadsheet.	
			3c Interpret mystery graphs.	
			3d Write algebraic expressions to represent situations.	
			3e Evaluate algebraic expressions and formulas.	
			3f Mentally add 1-digit integers.	
			3g Represent rates with formulas, tables, and graphs.	
			3h Convert between fractions and mixed numbers.	
			3i Find the least common multiple of two numbers.	
			3j Find the greatest common factor of two numbers.	

Notes to Parents

Copyright © SRA/McGraw-Hill

B = Beginning; **D** = Developing; **S** = Secure

Use with Lesson 3.11.

439

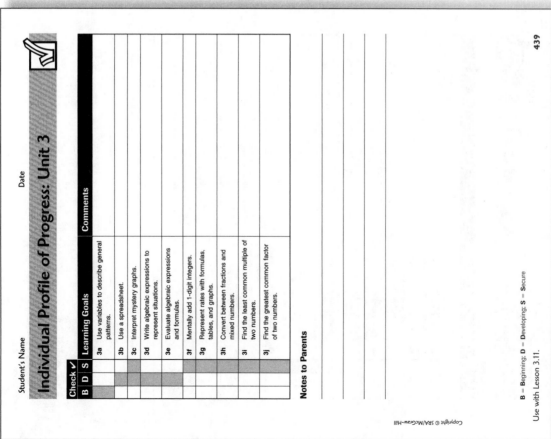

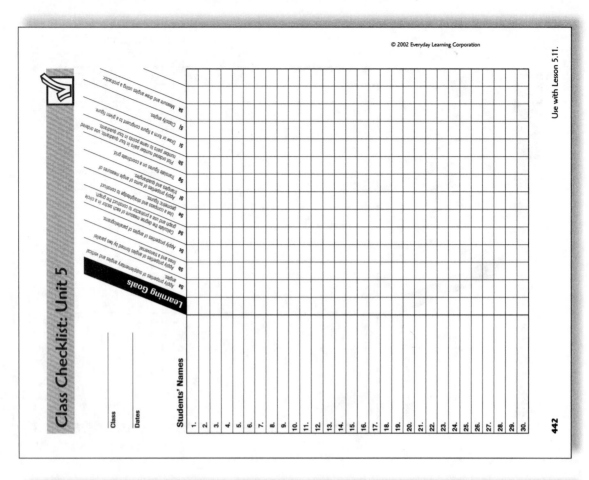

Class Checklist: Unit 5

© 2002 Everyday Learning Corporation

Learning Goals

- 5a Apply properties of supplementary angles and vertical angles.
- 5b Apply properties of angles formed by two parallel lines and a transversal.
- 5c Apply properties of angles of parallelograms.
- 5d Calculate the degree measure of each sector in a circle graph and use a protractor to construct the graph.
- 5e Use a compass and straightedge to construct geometric figures.
- 5f Apply properties of sums of angle measures of triangles and quadrilaterals.
- 5g Translate figures on a coordinate grid.
- 5h Plot ordered number pairs in four quadrants; use ordered number pairs to name points in four quadrants.
- 5i Draw or form a figure congruent to a given figure.
- 5j Classify angles.
- 5k Measure and draw angles using a protractor.

Class _____

Dates _____

Students' Names

1.
2.
3.
4.
5.
6.
7.
8.
9.
10.
11.
12.
13.
14.
15.
16.
17.
18.
19.
20.
21.
22.
23.
24.
25.
26.
27.
28.
29.
30.

Use with Lesson 5.11.

442

Student's Name _____ Date _____

Individual Profile of Progress: Unit 4

Check ✔ B	D	S		Learning Goals	Comments
			4a	Construct circle graphs with the Percent Circle.	
			4b	Use an algorithm to multiply fractions and mixed numbers.	
			4c	Use an algorithm to add and subtract mixed numbers having fractions with unlike denominators.	
			4d	Use an algorithm to subtract mixed numbers having fractions with like denominators.	
			4e	Find a percent of a number.	
			4f	Use an algorithm to add mixed numbers having fractions with like denominators.	
			4g	Use an algorithm to add and subtract fractions with like and unlike denominators.	
			4h	Compare and order fractions.	
			4i	Convert between fractions, mixed numbers, decimals, and percents.	
			4j	Write fractions and mixed numbers in simplest form.	

Notes to Parents

_____

B = Beginning; D = Developing; S = Secure

Use with Lesson 4.12.

Copyright © SRA/McGraw-Hill

441

Class Checklist: Unit 6

Copyright © SRA/McGraw–Hill

Class _____

Dates _____

Learning Goals

6a Solve and graph solutions for inequalities.

6b Solve equations.

6c Use an algorithm to add, subtract, multiply, and divide fractions and mixed numbers.

6d Find opposites and reciprocals of numbers.

6e Add, subtract, multiply, and divide integers.

6f Understand and apply order of operations to evaluate expressions and solve number sentences.

6g Determine whether number sentences are true or false.

6h Compare and order integers.

6i Understand and apply the identity property for multiplication.

6j Understand and apply the commutative property for addition and multiplication.

6k Understand and apply the associative property for addition and multiplication.

Students' Names

1.
2.
3.
4.
5.
6.
7.
8.
9.
10.
11.
12.
13.
14.
15.
16.
17.
18.
19.
20.
21.
22.
23.
24.
25.
26.
27.
28.
29.
30.

444

Use with Lesson 6.13.

Student's Name _____ Date _____

Individual Profile of Progress: Unit 5

Check ✔			Learning Goals	Comments
B	D	S		
			5a Apply properties of supplementary angles and vertical angles.	
			5b Apply properties of angles formed by two parallel lines and a transversal.	
			5c Apply properties of angles of parallelograms.	
			5d Calculate the degree measure of each sector in a circle graph and use a protractor to construct the graph.	
			5e Use a compass and straightedge to construct geometric figures.	
			5f Apply properties of sums of angle measures of triangles and quadrangles.	
			5g Translate figures on a coordinate grid.	
			5h Plot ordered number pairs in four quadrants; use ordered number pairs to name points in four quadrants.	
			5i Draw or form a figure congruent to a given figure.	
			5j Classify angles.	
			5k Measure and draw angles using a protractor.	

Notes to Parents

B = Beginning; D = Developing; S = Secure

Use with Lesson 5.11.

443

Copyright © SRA/McGraw–Hill

Class Checklist: Unit 7

Copyright © SRA/McGraw-Hill

Class _____

Dates _____

Learning Goals

- 7a Understand and use tree diagrams to solve problems.
- 7b Construct and interpret Venn diagrams.
- 7c Calculate probability in simple situations.
- 7d Understand what constitutes a fair game.
- 7e Understand and apply the concept of random numbers to probability situations.
- 7f Solve "fraction-of-a-fraction" problems.
- 7g Understand how sample size affects results.

Students' Names

1.
2.
3.
4.
5.
6.
7.
8.
9.
10.
11.
12.
13.
14.
15.
16.
17.
18.
19.
20.
21.
22.
23.
24.
25.
26.
27.
28.
29.
30.

Use with Lesson 7.9.

446

Student's Name _____   Date _____

Individual Profile of Progress: Unit 6

Check ✔			Learning Goals	Comments
B	**D**	**S**		
			6a Solve and graph solutions for inequalities.	
			6b Solve equations.	
			6c Use an algorithm to add, subtract, multiply, and divide fractions and mixed numbers.	
			6d Find opposites and reciprocals of numbers.	
			6e Add, subtract, multiply, and divide integers.	
			6f Understand and apply order of operations to evaluate expressions and solve number sentences.	
			6g Determine whether number sentences are true or false.	
			6h Compare and order integers.	
			6i Understand and apply the identity property for multiplication.	
			6j Understand and apply the commutative property for addition and multiplication.	
			6k Understand and apply the associative property for addition and multiplication.	

Notes to Parents

_____

_____

_____

Copyright © SRA/McGraw-Hill

B = Beginning; D = Developing; S = Secure

Use with Lesson 6.13.

445

Class Checklist: Unit 8

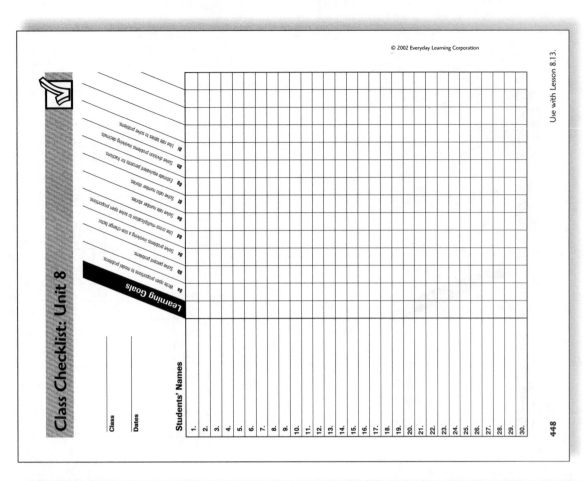

© 2002 Everyday Learning Corporation

Class _____

Dates _____

Learning Goals

8a	Write open proportions to model problems.
8b	Solve percent problems.
8c	Solve problems involving a size-change factor.
8d	Use cross-multiplication to solve open proportions.
8e	Solve ratio number stories.
8f	Solve ratio number stories.
8g	Estimate equivalent percents for fractions.
8h	Solve division problems involving decimals.
8i	Use rate tables to solve problems.

Students' Names

1.
2.
3.
4.
5.
6.
7.
8.
9.
10.
11.
12.
13.
14.
15.
16.
17.
18.
19.
20.
21.
22.
23.
24.
25.
26.
27.
28.
29.
30.

Use with Lesson 8.13.

448

Individual Profile of Progress: Unit 7

Student's Name _____ Date _____

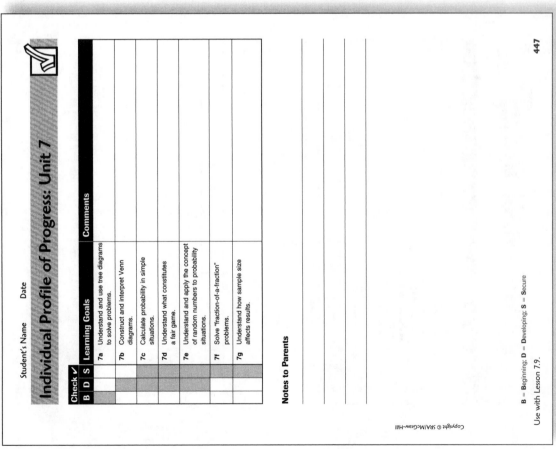

Check ✔			Learning Goals	Comments
B	D	S		
			7a	Understand and use tree diagrams to solve problems.	
			7b	Construct and interpret Venn diagrams.	
			7c	Calculate probability in simple situations.	
			7d	Understand what constitutes a fair game.	
			7e	Understand and apply the concept of random numbers to probability situations.	
			7f	Solve "fraction-of-a-fraction" problems.	
			7g	Understand how sample size affects results.	

Notes to Parents

_____

_____

_____

_____

B = Beginning; **D** = Developing; **S** = Secure

Use with Lesson 7.9.

447

Copyright © SRA/McGraw-Hill

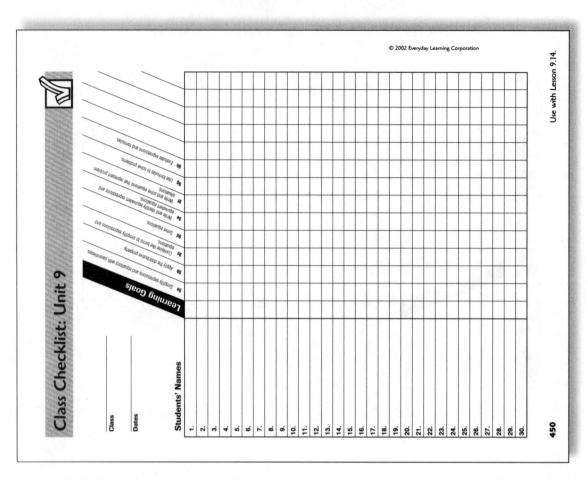

Class Checklist: Unit 9

Class _____

Dates _____

Learning Goals

- **9a** Simplify expressions and equations with parentheses.
- **9b** Apply the distributive property.
- **9c** Combine like terms to simplify expressions and equations.
- **9d** Solve equations.
- **9e** Write and identify equivalent expressions and equivalent equations.
- **9f** Write and solve equations that represent problem situations.
- **9g** Use formulas to solve problems.
- **9h** Evaluate expressions and formulas.

Students' Names

1.
2.
3.
4.
5.
6.
7.
8.
9.
10.
11.
12.
13.
14.
15.
16.
17.
18.
19.
20.
21.
22.
23.
24.
25.
26.
27.
28.
29.
30.

© 2002 Everyday Learning Corporation

Use with Lesson 9.14.

450

Student's Name _____ Date _____

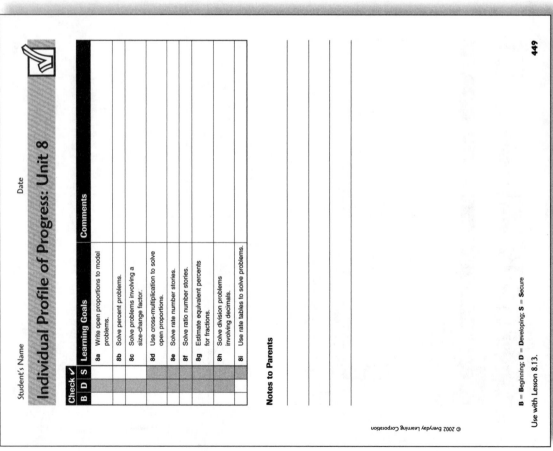

Individual Profile of Progress: Unit 8

Check ✓			Learning Goals	Comments
B	**D**	**S**		
			8a Write open proportions to model problems.	
			8b Solve percent problems.	
			8c Solve problems involving a size-change factor.	
			8d Use cross-multiplication to solve open proportions.	
			8e Solve rate number stories.	
			8f Solve ratio number stories.	
			8g Estimate equivalent percents for fractions.	
			8h Solve division problems involving decimals.	
			8i Use rate tables to solve problems.	

Notes to Parents _____

B = Beginning; **D** = Developing; **S** = Secure

Use with Lesson 8.13.

© 2002 Everyday Learning Corporation

449

Class Checklist: Unit 10

© 2002 Everyday Learning Corporation

Class _____

Dates _____

Learning Goals

- **10a** Identify and use notation for semiregular tessellations.
- **10b** Identify regular tessellations.
- **10c** Create nonpolygonal, translation tessellations.
- **10d** Create nonpolygonal, translation tessellations.
- **10e** Explore rotation and point symmetry.
- **10f** Discover properties of solids.
- **10f** Perform topological transformations.

Students' Names

1.
2.
3.
4.
5.
6.
7.
8.
9.
10.
11.
12.
13.
14.
15.
16.
17.
18.
19.
20.
21.
22.
23.
24.
25.
26.
27.
28.
29.
30.

Use with Lesson 10.7.

452

Student's Name _____ Date _____

Individual Profile of Progress: Unit 9

Check ✔ B D S	Learning Goals	Comments
	9a Simplify expressions and equations with parentheses.	
	9b Apply the distributive property.	
	9c Combine like terms to simplify expressions and equations.	
	9d Solve equations.	
	9e Write and identify equivalent expressions and equivalent equations.	
	9f Write and solve equations that represent problem situations.	
	9g Use formulas to solve problems.	
	9h Evaluate expressions and formulas.	

Notes to Parents

_____

_____

_____

B = Beginning; **D** = Developing; **S** = Secure

Use with Lesson 9.14.

© 2002 Everyday Learning Corporation

451

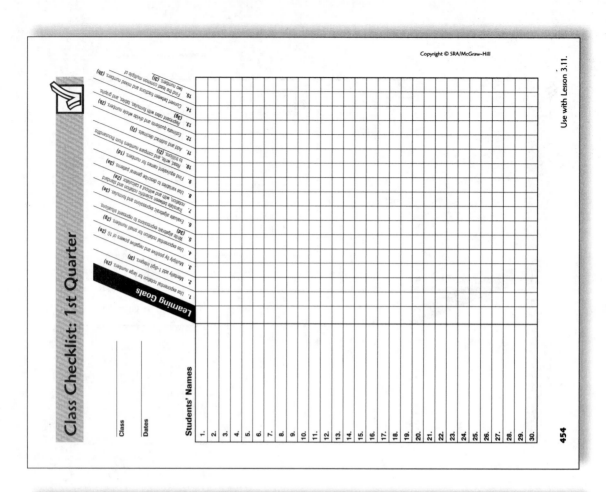

Class Checklist: 1st Quarter

Class

Dates

Learning Goals

1. Use exponential notation for large numbers. (2h)
2. Mentally add 1-digit integers. (3n)
3. Multiply by positive and negative powers of 10. (2e)
4. Use exponential notation for small numbers. (2e)
5. Write negative exponents. (2g)
6. Use algebraic expressions to represent situations. (3d)
7. Translate between algebraic expressions and formulas.
8. Evaluate algebraic expressions and formulas. (3c)
9. Use variables to describe general patterns. (3a)
   Find equivalent names for numbers. (3a)
10. Read, write, and compare numbers from thousandths to trillions. (2j)
11. Add and subtract decimals. (2j)
12. Estimate quotients and divide whole numbers. (2g)
13. Represent rates with formulas, tables, and graphs. (2x)
14. Convert between fractions and mixed numbers. (2c)
    Find the least common multiple of two numbers. (3j)
15.

Students' Names
1.
2.
3.
4.
5.
6.
7.
8.
9.
10.
11.
12.
13.
14.
15.
16.
17.
18.
19.
20.
21.
22.
23.
24.
25.
26.
27.
28.
29.
30.

Copyright © SRA/McGraw-Hill

Use with Lesson 3.11.

454

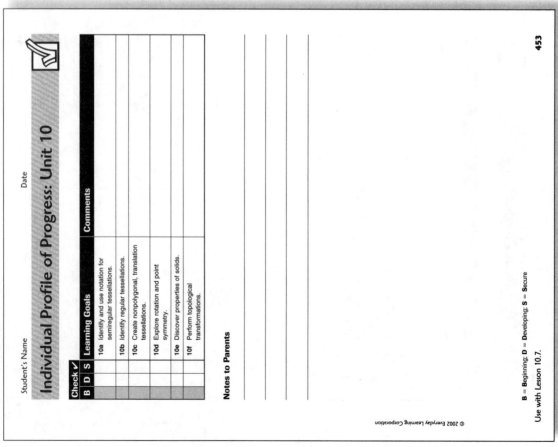

Student's Name

Date

Individual Profile of Progress: Unit 10

Check ✓			Learning Goals	Comments
B	D	S		
			10a Identify and use notation for semiregular tessellations.	
			10b Identify regular tessellations.	
			10c Create nonpolygonal, translation tessellations.	
			10d Explore rotation and point symmetry.	
			10e Discover properties of solids.	
			10f Perform topological transformations.	

Notes to Parents

B = Beginning; **D** = Developing; **S** = Secure

Use with Lesson 10.7.

© 2002 Everyday Learning Corporation

453

Student's Name _____ Date _____

Individual Profile of Progress: 1st Quarter

© 2002 Everyday Learning Corporation

Check ✔			Learning Goals	Comments
B	**D**	**S**		
			1. Use exponential notation for large numbers. **(2h)**	
			2. Mentally add 1-digit positive and negative numbers. **(3f)**	
			3. Multiply by positive and negative powers of 10. **(2e)**	
			4. Use exponential notation for small numbers. **(2g)**	
			5. Write algebraic expressions to represent situations. **(3d)**	
			6. Evaluate algebraic expressions. **(3e)**	
			7. Translate between scientific notation and standard notation, with and without a calculator. **(2a)**	
			8. Use variables to describe general patterns. **(3a)**	
			9. Find equivalent names for numbers. **(1d)**	
			10. Read, write, and compare numbers from thousandths to trillions. **(2l)**	
			11. Add and subtract decimals. **(2j)**	
			12. Estimate quotients and divide whole numbers. **(2k)**	
			13. Represent rates with formulas, tables, and graphs. **(3g)**	
			14. Convert between fractions and mixed numbers. **(3h)**	
			15. Find the least common multiple of two numbers. **(3i)**	
			16. Find the greatest common factor of two numbers. **(3j)**	
			17. Estimate products and multiply decimals. **(2b)**	
			18. Divide two whole numbers; give the answer to a specified number of decimal places. **(2c)**	

B = Beginning; **D** = Developing; **S** = Secure

456

Use with Lesson 3.11.

Class Checklist: 1st Quarter (cont.)

Class _____

Dates _____

Learning Goals

16. Find the greatest common factor of two numbers. **(3j)**
17. Estimate products and multiply decimals. **(2b)**
18. Divide two whole numbers; give the answer to a specified number of decimal places. **(2c)**
19. Estimate the quotient and divide a decimal by a whole number. **(2d)**
20. Interpret number-and-word notation for large numbers. **(2f)**
21. Identify landmarks of data sets. **(1e)**
22. Compute and understand the mean. **(1f)**
23. Interpret and construct broken-line graphs. **(1g)**
24. Use a Percent Circle to interpret circle graphs. **(1h)**
25. Interpret and construct bar graphs. **(1h)**
26. Use a spreadsheet. **(3b)**
27. Use a Percent Circle to interpret circle graphs. **(1c)**
28. Interpret mystery graphs. **(1b, 3c)**
29. Interpret and construct step graphs. **(1a)**

Students' Names

1.
2.
3.
4.
5.
6.
7.
8.
9.
10.
11.
12.
13.
14.
15.
16.
17.
18.
19.
20.
21.
22.
23.
24.
25.
26.
27.
28.
29.
30.

Copyright © SRA/McGraw-Hill

455

Use with Lesson 3.11.

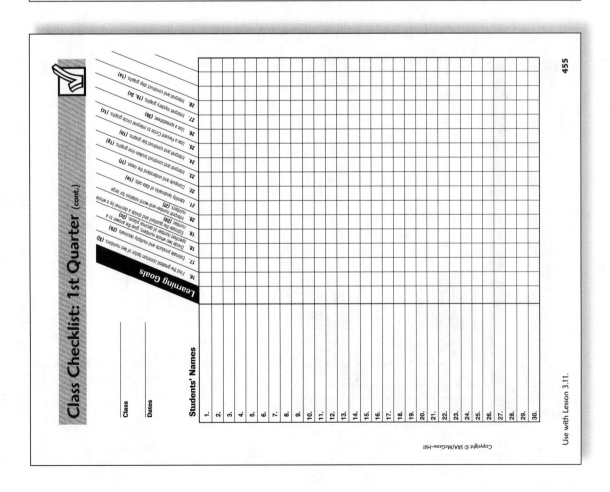

Class Checklist: 2nd Quarter

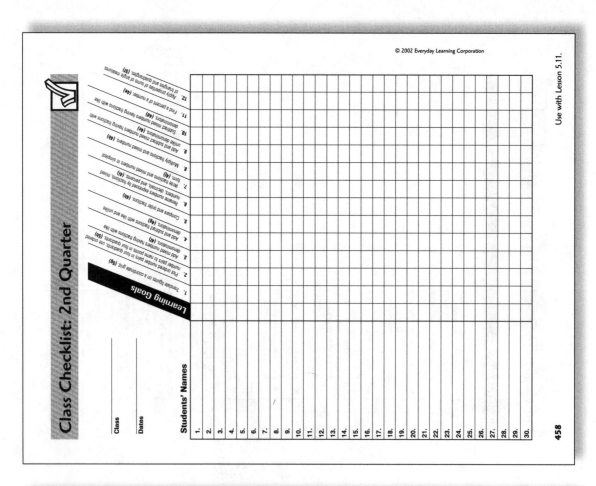

© 2002 Everyday Learning Corporation

Class _____

Dates _____

Learning Goals

1. Translate figures on a coordinate grid. **(5g)**
2. Plot ordered number pairs in four quadrants; use ordered number pairs to name points in four quadrants. **(5h)**
3. Add mixed numbers having fractions with like denominators. **(4h)**
4. Add and subtract fractions with like and unlike denominators. **(4g)**
5. Compare and order fractions. **(4f)**
6. Rename numbers expressed by fractions, mixed numbers, decimals, and percents. **(4j)**
7. Write fractions and mixed numbers in simplest form. **(4i)**
8. Multiply fractions and mixed numbers. **(4l)**
9. Add and subtract mixed numbers. **(4b)**
10. Subtract mixed numbers having fractions with unlike denominators. **(4e)**
11. Find a percent of a number. **(4a)**
12. Apply properties of sums of angle measures of triangles and quadrangles. **(5i)**

Students' Names

1.
2.
3.
4.
5.
6.
7.
8.
9.
10.
11.
12.
13.
14.
15.
16.
17.
18.
19.
20.
21.
22.
23.
24.
25.
26.
27.
28.
29.
30.

Use with Lesson 5.11.

458

Student's Name _____   Date _____

Individual Profile of Progress: 1st Quarter

Check ✓

B	D	S		Learning Goals	Comments
			19.	Estimate the quotient and divide a decimal by a whole number. **(2d)**	
			20.	Interpret number-and-word notation for large numbers. **(2f)**	
			21.	Identify landmarks of data sets. **(1e)**	
			22.	Compute and understand the mean. **(1f)**	
			23.	Interpret and construct broken-line graphs. **(1g)**	
			24.	Interpret and construct bar graphs. **(1h)**	
			25.	Use a Percent Circle to interpret circle graphs. **(1c)**	
			26.	Match mystery line plots with descriptions. **(1b)**	
			27.	Use a spreadsheet. **(3b)**	
			28.	Interpret mystery graphs. **(3c)**	
			29.	Interpret and construct step graphs. **(1a)**	

Notes to Parents

B = Beginning; D = Developing; S = Secure

Use with Lesson 3.11.

© 2002 Everyday Learning Corporation

457

Individual Profile of Progress: 2nd Quarter

Student's Name _____ Date _____

Copyright © SRA/McGraw-Hill

Check ✓ B = Beginning; D = Developing; S = Secure

	Learning Goals	Comments
1.	Translate figures on a coordinate grid. (5g)	
2.	Plot ordered number pairs in four quadrants; use ordered number pairs to name points in four quadrants. (5h)	
3.	Use an algorithm to add mixed numbers having fractions with like denominators. (4f)	
4.	Use an algorithm to add and subtract fractions with like and unlike denominators. (4g)	
5.	Compare and order fractions. (4h)	
6.	Convert between fractions, mixed numbers, decimals, and percents. (4i)	
7.	Write fractions and mixed numbers in simplest form. (4j)	
8.	Use an algorithm to multiply fractions and mixed numbers. (4b)	
9.	Use an algorithm to add and subtract mixed numbers having fractions with unlike denominators. (4c)	
10.	Use an algorithm to subtract mixed numbers having fractions with like denominators. (4d)	
11.	Find a percent of a number. (4e)	
12.	Apply properties of sums of angle measures of triangles and quadrangles. (5f)	
13.	Draw or form a figure congruent to a given figure. (5i)	
14.	Classify angles. (5l)	
15.	Measure and draw angles using a protractor. (5k)	
16.	Apply properties of supplementary angles and vertical angles. (5a)	
17.	Apply properties of angles formed by two parallel lines and a transversal. (5b)	
18.	Apply properties of angles of parallelograms. (5c)	
19.	Use a compass and straightedge to construct geometric figures. (5e)	
20.	Construct circle graphs with the Percent Circle. (4a)	
21.	Calculate the degree measure of each sector in a circle graph and use a protractor to construct the graph. (5d)	

B = Beginning; D = Developing; S = Secure

460   Use with Lesson 5.11.

Class Checklist: 2nd Quarter (cont.)

Class _____

Dates _____

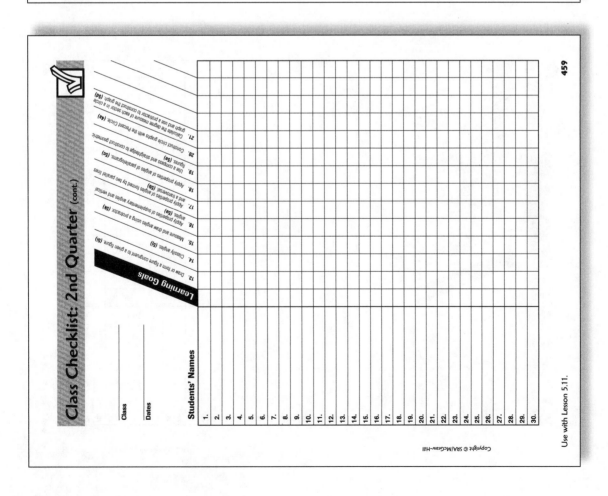

Learning Goals

13. Draw or form a figure congruent to a given figure. (5i)
14. Classify angles. (5l)
15. Measure and draw angles using a protractor. (5k)
16. Apply properties of supplementary angles and vertical angles. (5a)
17. Apply properties of angles formed by two parallel lines and a transversal. (5b)
18. Apply properties of angles of parallelograms. (5c)
19. Use a compass and straightedge to construct geometric figures. (5e)
20. Construct circle graphs with the Percent Circle. (4a)
21. Calculate the degree measure of each sector in a circle graph and use a protractor to construct the graph. (5d)

Students' Names

1–30.

Copyright © SRA/McGraw-Hill

459   Use with Lesson 5.11.

Class Checklist: 3rd Quarter (cont.)

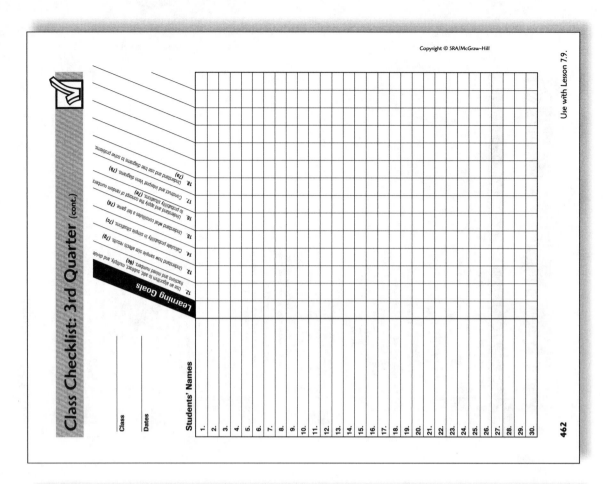

Class _____

Dates _____

Learning Goals

12. Use an algorithm to add, subtract, multiply, and divide fractions and mixed numbers. (6e)
13. Understand how sample size affects results. (7a)
14. Calculate probability in simple situations. (7a)
15. Understand what constitutes a fair game. (7d)
16. Understand and apply the concept of random numbers to probability situations. (7a)
17. Construct and interpret Venn diagrams. (7b)
18. Understand and use tree diagrams to solve problems. (7a)

Students' Names

1.
2.
3.
4.
5.
6.
7.
8.
9.
10.
11.
12.
13.
14.
15.
16.
17.
18.
19.
20.
21.
22.
23.
24.
25.
26.
27.
28.
29.
30.

Copyright © SRA/McGraw-Hill

462

Use with Lesson 7.9.

Class Checklist: 3rd Quarter

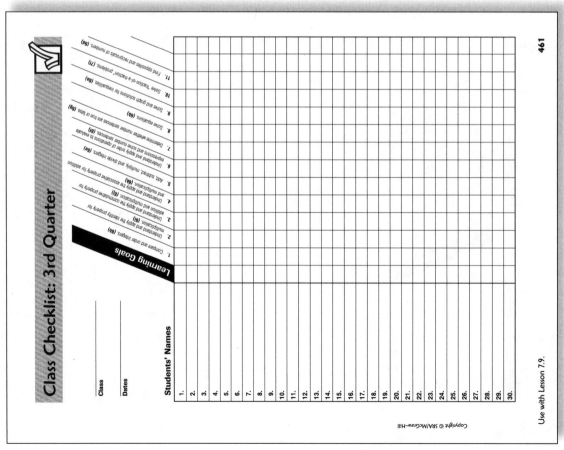

Class _____

Dates _____

Learning Goals

1. Compare and order integers. (6h)
2. Understand and apply the identity property for multiplication. (6f)
3. Understand and apply the commutative property for addition and multiplication. (6f)
4. Understand and apply the associative property for addition and multiplication. (6f)
5. Add, subtract, multiply, and divide integers. (6g)
6. Understand and apply order of operations to evaluate expressions and solve number sentences. (6i)
7. Determine whether number sentences are true or false. (6i)
8. Solve equations. (6g)
9. Solve equations. (6g)
10. Solve and graph solutions for inequalities. (6a)
11. Solve "fraction-of-a-fraction" problems. (7f)
12. Find opposites and reciprocals of numbers. (6d)

Students' Names

1.
2.
3.
4.
5.
6.
7.
8.
9.
10.
11.
12.
13.
14.
15.
16.
17.
18.
19.
20.
21.
22.
23.
24.
25.
26.
27.
28.
29.
30.

461

Copyright © SRA/McGraw-Hill

Use with Lesson 7.9.

Class Checklist: 4th Quarter

Class _____

Dates _____

© 2002 Everyday Learning Corporation

Learning Goals

1. Evaluate expressions and formulas. (9h)
2. Apply the distributive property. (9b)
3. Combine like terms to simplify expressions and equations. (9c)
4. Solve equations. (9d)
5. Write and identify equivalent expressions and equations. (9e)
6. Write and solve equations that represent problem situations. (9f)
7. Use formulas to solve problems. (9i)
8. Simplify expressions and equations with parentheses. (9g)
9. Use rate tables to solve problems. (9j)
10. Use cross-multiplication to solve open proportions. (9a)
11. Solve rate number stories. (9k)
12. Solve ratio number stories. (9l)

Students' Names

1.
2.
3.
4.
5.
6.
7.
8.
9.
10.
11.
12.
13.
14.
15.
16.
17.
18.
19.
20.
21.
22.
23.
24.
25.
26.
27.
28.
29.
30.

Use with Lesson 10.7.

464

Student's Name _____ Date _____

Individual Profile of Progress: 3rd Quarter

Check ✔			Learning Goals	Comments
B	D	S		
			1. Compare and order integers. (6h)	
			2. Understand and apply the identity property for multiplication. (6i)	
			3. Understand and apply the commutative property for addition and multiplication. (6j)	
			4. Understand and apply the associative property for addition and multiplication. (6k)	
			5. Add, subtract, multiply, and divide integers. (6e)	
			6. Understand and apply order of operations to evaluate expressions and solve number sentences. (6f)	
			7. Determine whether number sentences are true or false. (6g)	
			8. Solve equations. (6b)	
			9. Solve and graph solutions for inequalities. (6a)	
			10. Solve "fraction-of-a-fraction" problems. (7f)	
			11. Find opposites and reciprocals of numbers. (6d)	
			12. Use an algorithm to add, subtract, multiply, and divide fractions and mixed numbers. (6c)	
			13. Understand how sample size affects results. (7g)	
			14. Calculate probability in simple situations. (7c)	
			15. Understand what constitutes a fair game. (7d)	
			16. Understand and apply the concept of random numbers to probability situations. (7e)	
			17. Construct and interpret Venn diagrams. (7b)	
			18. Understand and use tree diagrams to solve problems. (7a)	

B = Beginning; D = Developing; S = Secure

Copyright © SRA/McGraw-Hill

Use with Lesson 7.9.

463

Student's Name _____ Date _____

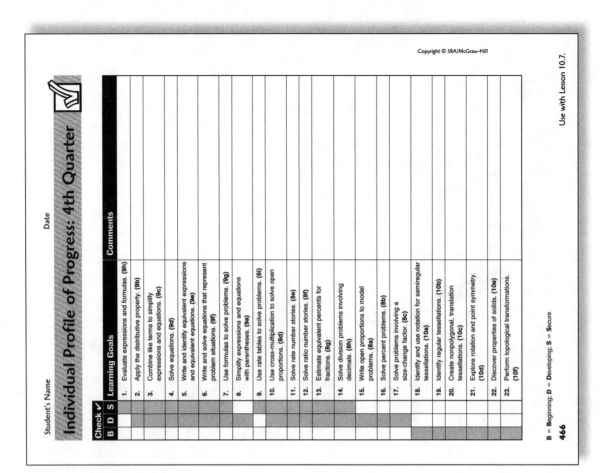

Individual Profile of Progress: 4th Quarter

Check ✔			Learning Goals	Comments
B	**D**	**S**		
			1. Evaluate expressions and formulas. **(9h)**	
			2. Apply the distributive property. **(9b)**	
			3. Combine like terms to simplify expressions and equations. **(9c)**	
			4. Solve equations. **(9d)**	
			5. Write and identify equivalent expressions and equivalent equations. **(9e)**	
			6. Write and solve equations that represent problem situations. **(9f)**	
			7. Use formulas to solve problems. **(9g)**	
			8. Simplify expressions and equations with parentheses. **(9a)**	
			9. Use rate tables to solve problems. **(8i)**	
			10. Use cross-multiplication to solve open proportions. **(8d)**	
			11. Solve rate number stories. **(8e)**	
			12. Solve ratio number stories. **(8f)**	
			13. Estimate equivalent percents for fractions. **(8g)**	
			14. Solve division problems involving decimals. **(8h)**	
			15. Write open proportions to model problems. **(8a)**	
			16. Solve percent problems. **(8b)**	
			17. Solve problems involving a size-change factor. **(8c)**	
			18. Identify and use notation for semiregular tessellations. **(10a)**	
			19. Identify regular tessellations. **(10b)**	
			20. Create nonpolygonal, translation tessellations. **(10c)**	
			21. Explore rotation and point symmetry. **(10d)**	
			22. Discover properties of solids. **(10e)**	
			23. Perform topological transformations. **(10f)**	

B = Beginning; **D** = Developing; **S** = Secure

466

Copyright © SRA/McGraw-Hill

Use with Lesson 10.7.

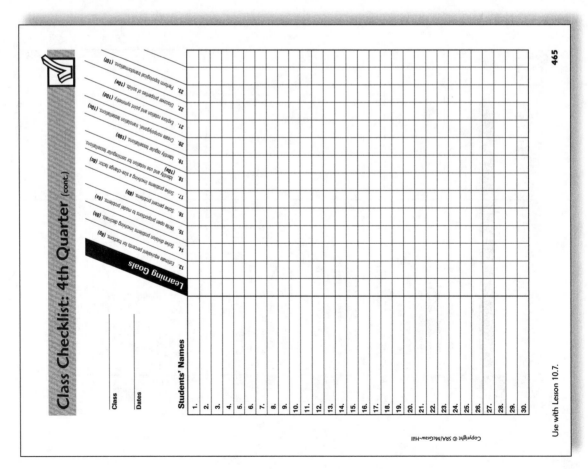

Class Checklist: 4th Quarter (cont.)

Class _____

Dates _____

Students' Names	13. Estimate equivalent percents for fractions. (8g)	14. Solve division problems involving decimals. (8h)	15. Write open proportions to model problems. (8a)	16. Solve percent problems. (8b)	17. Solve problems involving a size-change factor. (8c)	18. Identify and use notation for semiregular tessellations (10a)	19. Identify regular tessellations (10b)	20. Create nonpolygonal, translation tessellations. (10c)	21. Explore rotation and point symmetry. (10d)	22. Discover properties of solids. (10e)	23. Perform topological transformations. (10f)
1.											
2.											
3.											
4.											
5.											
6.											
7.											
8.											
9.											
10.											
11.											
12.											
13.											
14.											
15.											
16.											
17.											
18.											
19.											
20.											
21.											
22.											
23.											
24.											
25.											
26.											
27.											
28.											
29.											
30.											

Learning Goals

Copyright © SRA/McGraw-Hill

465

Use with Lesson 10.7.

List of Assessment Sources

Ongoing Assessment

Product Assessment

Periodic Assessment

Outside Tests

Other

Use as needed.

© 2002 Everyday Learning Corporation

467

Student's Name _____ Date _____

Individual Profile of Progress

Check ✔			Learning Goals	Comments
B	D	S		
			1.	
			2.	
			3.	
			4.	
			5.	
			6.	
			7.	
			8.	
			9.	
			10.	

Notes to Parents

B = Beginning; D = Developing; S = Secure

© 2002 Everyday Learning Corporation

Use as needed.

468

Class Progress Indicator

© 2002 Everyday Learning Corporation

Mathematical Topic Being Assessed: _____

	BEGINNING	DEVELOPING OR DEVELOPING+	SECURE OR SECURE+
First Assessment After Lesson: ____ Dates included: ____ to ____			
Second Assessment After Lesson: ____ Dates included: ____ to ____			
Third Assessment After Lesson: ____ Dates included: ____ to ____			

Notes _____

_____

_____

Use as needed.

470

Class Checklist

Class _____

Dates _____

Learning Goals

Students' Names

1.
2.
3.
4.
5.
6.
7.
8.
9.
10.
11.
12.
13.
14.
15.
16.
17.
18.
19.
20.
21.
22.
23.
24.
25.
26.
27.
28.
29.
30.

© 2002 Everyday Learning Corporation

Use as needed.

469

Name _____ Date _____

My Math Class

Interest Inventory

1. In math class, I am good at _____

_____

_____

2. One thing I like about math is _____

_____

3. One thing I find difficult in mathematics class is _____

_____

4. The most interesting thing I have learned in math so far this year is

_____

_____

5. Outside school, I used mathematics when I _____

_____

6. I would like to know more about _____

_____

© 2002 Everyday Learning Corporation

Use as needed.

Name _____ Date _____

Evaluating My Math Class

Interest Inventory

Dislike a Lot	Dislike	Neither Like nor Dislike	Like	Like a Lot
1	2	3	4	5

Use the scale above to describe how you feel about:

1. your math class.

2. working with a partner or in a group.

3. working by yourself.

4. solving problems.

5. making up problems for others to solve.

6. finding new ways to solve problems.

7. challenges in math class.

8. playing mathematical games.

9. working on Study Links.

10. working on projects that take more than a day to complete.

11. Which math lesson has been your favorite so far? Why?

_____

_____

_____

_____

© 2002 Everyday Learning Corporation

Use as needed.

Math Log

Name

Date

© 2002 Everyday Learning Corporation

Use as needed.

474

Weekly Math Log

Name

Date

1. What did you study in math this week?

2. Many ideas in math are related to other ideas within math. Think about how the topic(s) you studied in class this week relate to other topics you learned before.

Your reflection can include what you learned in previous years.

Use as needed.

© 2002 Everyday Learning Corporation

473

Sample Math Work

© 2002 Everyday Learning Corporation

Name _____ Date _____

Self-Assessment

Attach a sample of your work to this form.

1. This work is an example of:

_____

_____

_____

_____

_____

_____

_____

2. This work shows that I can:

_____

_____

_____

_____

OPTIONAL

3. This work shows that I still need to improve:

_____

_____

_____

Use as needed.

476

Number-Story Math Log

Name _____ Date _____

1. Write an easy number story that uses mathematical ideas that you have studied recently. Solve the problem.

Number Story _____

_____

_____

Solution _____

2. Write a difficult number story that uses mathematical ideas that you have studied recently. If you can, solve the number story. If you are not able to solve it, explain what you need to know to solve it.

Number Story _____

_____

_____

Solution _____

© 2002 Everyday Learning Corporation

Use as needed.

475

Name

Exit Slip

Date

Time

Name

Exit Slip

Date

Time

© 2002 Everyday Learning Corporation

Use as needed.

478

Name

Date

Discussion of My Math Work

Self-Assessment

Attach a sample of your work to this page. Tell what you think is important about your sample.

© 2002 Everyday Learning Corporation

Use as needed.

477

Glossary

anecdotal records Brief, pertinent pieces of information gathered during informal observation.

assessment The gathering of information about students' progress. This might include their knowledge and use of mathematics, as well as their feelings about their mathematical progress. This information is used to draw conclusions for individual and class instruction.

assessment plan A balanced group of assessment activities chosen by an individual teacher.

assessment sources Mathematical tasks or interactions that can be used for gathering data for assessment purposes.

Class Checklist A tool used to record ongoing observations and interactions.

Class Progress Indicator A form upon which the results of sequential assessment tasks for various mathematical ideas, routines, concepts, and so on, can be recorded for the whole class during the school year using such categories as Beginning, Developing, and Secure.

concepts Basic mathematical ideas that are fundamental in guiding reasoning and problem solving in unfamiliar situations.

evaluation Judgments based on information gathered during assessment.

Individual Profile of Progress A recording tool used to measure the progress of individual students on specific learning goals.

interest inventories Written formats for assessing students' attitudes toward mathematics.

interviews Conversations between a teacher and individual students in which the teacher can obtain information useful for assessing mathematical progress.

long-term projects Mathematical activities that may require time spans of days, weeks, or months to complete.

math logs Records of a student's mathematical thinking through writing, pictures, diagrams, and so on.

observation Watching and recording students' interactions and communications during regular instructional activities.

Ongoing Assessment The gathering of assessment data during regular instructional activities, mostly through observation.

open-ended questions Questions that have multiple answers and strategies for arriving at the answers. (Open-ended questions are good assessments for problem solving and reasoning.)

Outside Tests Usually tests at the school, district, or state level, or nationally standardized tests. If these tests do not match the curriculum, they may not provide valid assessment information.

performance The carrying out or completing of a mathematical activity that displays a student's knowledge and judgment while he or she is engaged in the activity.

Periodic Assessment The more formal gathering of assessment information, often outside of regular instructional time. One example is end-of-unit assessments.

Portfolio A sample collection of a student's mathematical work and related writing representing his or her progress over the school year.

Product Assessment Samples of students' work, which may include pictures, diagrams, or concrete representations.

progress The growth, development, and continuous improvement of students' mathematical abilities.

Progress Indicator *See* Class Progress Indicator.

reflective writing The ability to reflect and write about mathematics as it relates to accomplishments, confidence, feelings, understanding or lack of understanding, goals, and so on.

representative work A piece of work that represents a student's ability and reflects a student's progress.

rubric A set of guidelines for scoring assessment activities. The most useful rubrics are those derived from experience with a wide variety of performances on an assessment task.

self-assessment The ability of students to judge, reflect on, acknowledge, and improve the quality of their mathematical thinking or productions.

standardized tests Typically, nationwide tests that are given, scored, and interpreted in a very consistent way, regardless of the population being tested.

strategies The thoughts and procedures an individual student uses to solve a problem.

validity of assessment The degree to which assessment data actually represent the knowledge, thought processes, and skills that students have attained.

Index

Lourdes Library
Gwynedd Mercy College
P. O. Box 901
Gwynedd Valley, PA 19437-0901

DISCARD

DISCARD
CURRICULUM COLLECTION